THE PROCLAMATION ON THE FAMILY

Other Books in the *Gospel Studies Series* by David J. Ridges

- Volume 1: Isaiah Made Easier
- Volume 2: The New Testament Made Easier, Part 1
- Volume 3: The New Testament Made Easier, Part 2

Upcoming volumes in the *Gospel Studies Series*:

- The Book of Mormon Made Easier (2004 release)
- The Doctrine & Covenants Made Easier (2005)
- The Pearl of Great Price Made Easier (2006)
- The Old Testament Made Easier— Selections from the Old Testament (2006)

Additional upcoming titles by David J. Ridges:

- 50 Signs of the Times and the Second Coming (2003)
- From Premortality to Exaltation: Doctrinal Details of the Plan of Salvation (2004)

Watch for these titles to also become available through Cedar Fort as e-books and on CD.

THE PROCLAMATION ON THE FAMILY

THE WORD OF THE LORD ON MORE THAN THIRTY CURRENT ISSUES

BY DAVID J. RIDGES

Springville, Utah

ISBN: 1-55517-716-6
e.2

Published by Bonneville Books
Imprint of Cedar Fort Inc.
www.cedarfort.com

Distributed by:

Cover design by Nicole Cunningham
Cover design © 2003 by Lyle Mortimer

Printed in the United States of America
10 9 8 7 6 5 4 3 2 1

Printed on acid-free paper

Library of Congress Control Number: 2003110345

Occasionally, members of the Church express a wish to have lived in the days of the Prophet Joseph Smith when so many revelations were given by the Lord. But we, too, live in a day where many revelations are being given by Him. And "The Family: A Proclamation to the World" is a marvelous document, a treasury of the revealed word of the Lord on a great many current issues which face our world.

Over a number of years of teaching, I have found students and adult members of the Church to be fascinated and surprised that so many current issues are addressed in this proclamation on the family. Therefore, the purpose of this book is to help members become more aware of the rather astonishing number of issues spoken of by the Lord through His servants in such a brief inspired document. It is hoped, also, that you will find other issues and counsel from the Savior not specifically pointed out in this volume.

The format used is intentionally simple. For each of the main chapters, a copy of the Proclamation is given with the specific issue addressed by the Lord bolded in order for the reader to see "at-a-glance" what was said on that particular topic. As you read, it becomes obvious that the Brethren were extremely careful in their choice of words to express the word and the will of the Lord on these issues. The term "Proclamation" has been used in this book to refer to "The Family: A Proclamation to the World."

My deepest thanks and appreciation go to my wife, Janette, and to Chad Daybell and the staff at Cedar Fort Incorporated for their help and encouragement in the completion of this book.

David J. Ridges

TABLE OF CONTENTS

THE FAMILY
A PROCLAMATION TO THE WORLD
THE FIRST PRESIDENCY AND COUNCIL OF THE TWELVE APOSTLES
OF THE CHURCH OF JESUS CHRIST OF LATTER-DAY SAINTS

We, the First Presidency and the council of the Twelve Apostles of The Church of Jesus Christ of Latter-day Saints, solemnly proclaim that marriage between a man and a woman is ordained of God and that the family is central to the Creator's plan for the eternal destiny of His children.

All human beings—male and female—are created in the image of God. Each is a beloved spirit son or daughter of heavenly parents, and, as such, each has a divine nature and destiny. Gender is an essential characteristic of individual premortal, mortal, and eternal identity and purpose.

In the premortal realm, spirit sons and daughters knew and worshiped God as their eternal Father and accepted His plan by which His children could obtain a physical body and gain earthly experience to progress toward perfection and ultimately realize his or her divine destiny as an heir of eternal life. The divine plan of happiness enables family relationships to be perpetuated beyond the grave. Sacred ordinances and covenants available in holy temples make it possible for individuals to return to the presence of God and for families to be united eternally.

The first commandment that God gave to Adam and Eve pertained to their potential for parenthood as husband and wife. We declare that God's commandment for His children to multiply and replenish the earth remains in force. We further declare that God has commanded that the sacred powers of procreation are to be employed only between man and woman, lawfully wedded as husband and wife.

We declare the means by which mortal life is created to be divinely appointed. We affirm the sanctity of life and of its importance in God's eternal plan.

Husband and wife have a solemn responsibility to love and care for each other and for their children. "Children are an heritage of the Lord." (Psalms 127:3.)

Parents have a sacred duty to rear their children in love and righteousness, to provide for their physical and spiritual needs, to teach them to love and serve one another, to observe the commandments of God and to be law-abiding citizens wherever they live. Husbands and wives—mothers and fathers—will be held accountable before God for the discharge of these obligations.

The family is ordained of God. Marriage between man and woman is essential to His eternal plan. Children are entitled to birth within the bonds of matrimony, and to be reared by a father and a mother who honor marital vows with complete fidelity. Happiness in family life is most likely to be achieved when founded upon the teachings of the Lord Jesus Christ. Successful marriages and families are established and maintained on principles of faith, prayer, repentance, forgiveness, respect, love, compassion, work, and wholesome recreational activities. By divine design, fathers are to preside over their families in love and righteousness and are responsible to provide the necessities of life and protection of their families. Mothers are primarily responsible for the nurture of their children. In these sacred responsibilities, fathers and mothers are obligated to help one another as equal partners. Disability, death, or other circumstances may necessitate individual adaptation. Extended families should lend support when needed.

We warn that individuals who violate covenants of chastity, who abuse spouse or offspring, or who fail to fulfill family responsibilities will one day stand accountable before God. Further, we warn that the disintegration of the family will bring upon individuals, communities, and nations the calamities foretold by ancient and modern prophets.

We call upon responsible citizens and officers of government everywhere to promote those measures designed to maintain and strengthen the family as the fundamental unit of society.

September 23, 1995

CHAPTER 1

"THE FAMILY: A PROCLAMATION TO THE WORLD" IS THE WORD OF THE LORD

In the April 1945 General Conference of the Church, Apostle Marion G. Romney, who would later serve for many years as a counselor in the First Presidency, said the following:

> "Today the Lord is revealing his will to all the inhabitants of the earth, and to members of the Church in particular, on the issues of this our day through the living prophets, with the First Presidency at the head. What they say as a presidency is what the Lord would say if He were here in person. This is the rock foundation of Mormonism. If it ever ceases to be the fact, this will be an apostate Church. . . So I repeat again, what the presidency say as a presidency is what the Lord would say if he were here, and it is scripture. It should be studied, understood, and followed, even as the revelations in the Doctrine and Covenants and other scriptures."

There is absolute safety for us in following the Brethren. It is a great source of security to have the word of the Lord on current issues. It brings stability, understanding and peace to the faithful. As we read and study this proclamation, we should treat it as scripture and apply it in our own lives. Also, we may be called upon to stand up for and gently explain these doctrines and truths as some around us find themselves confused as to what is right and what is wrong when they are caught up in the tides of public sentiment and debate.

A PROCLAMATION TO THE WORLD

THE FIRST PRESIDENCY AND COUNCIL OF THE TWELVE APOSTLES
OF THE CHURCH OF JESUS CHRIST OF LATTER-DAY SAINTS

We, the First Presidency and the council of the Twelve Apostles of The Church of Jesus Christ of Latter-day Saints, solemnly proclaim that marriage between a man and a woman is ordained of God and that the family is central to the Creator's plan for the eternal destiny of His children.

All human beings—male and female—are created in the image of God. Each is a beloved spirit son or daughter of heavenly parents, and, as such, each has a divine nature and destiny. Gender is an essential characteristic of individual premortal, mortal, and eternal identity and purpose.

In the premortal realm, spirit sons and daughters knew and worshiped God as their eternal Father and accepted His plan by which His children could obtain a physical body and gain earthly experience to progress toward perfection and ultimately realize his or her divine destiny as an heir of eternal life. The divine plan of happiness enables family relationships to be perpetuated beyond the grave. Sacred ordinances and covenants available in holy temples make it possible for individuals to return to the presence of God and for families to be united eternally.

The first commandment that God gave to Adam and Eve pertained to their potential for parenthood as husband and wife. We declare that God's commandment for His children to multiply and replenish the earth remains in force. We further declare that God has commanded that the sacred powers of procreation are to be employed only between man and woman, lawfully wedded as husband and wife.

We declare the means by which mortal life is created to be divinely appointed. We affirm the sanctity of life and of its importance in God's eternal plan.

Husband and wife have a solemn responsibility to love and care for each other and for their children. "Children are an heritage of the Lord." (Psalms 127:3.)

Parents have a sacred duty to rear their children in love and righteousness, to provide for their physical and spiritual needs, to teach them to love and serve one another, to observe the commandments of God and to be law-abiding citizens wherever they live. Husbands and wives—mothers and fathers—will be held accountable before God for the discharge of these obligations.

The family is ordained of God. Marriage between man and woman is essential to His eternal plan. Children are entitled to birth within the bonds of matrimony, and to be reared by a father and a mother who honor marital vows with complete fidelity. Happiness in family life is most likely to be achieved when founded upon the teachings of the Lord Jesus Christ. Successful marriages and families are established and maintained on principles of faith, prayer, repentance, forgiveness, respect, love, compassion, work, and wholesome recreational activities. By divine design, fathers are to preside over their families in love and righteousness and are responsible to provide the necessities of life and protection of their families. Mothers are primarily responsible for the nurture of their children. In these sacred responsibilities, fathers and mothers are obligated to help one another as equal partners. Disability, death, or other circumstances may necessitate individual adaptation. Extended families should lend support when needed.

We warn that individuals who violate covenants of chastity, who abuse spouse or offspring, or who fail to fulfill family responsibilities will one day stand accountable before God. Further, we warn that the disintegration of the family will bring upon individuals, communities, and nations the calamities foretold by ancient and modern prophets.

We call upon responsible citizens and officers of government everywhere to promote those measures designed to maintain and strengthen the family as the fundamental unit of society.

September 23, 1995

CHAPTER 2

THE ROLE OF "PROPHETS, SEERS, AND REVELATORS"

Before we consider specific issues addressed in the Proclamation, we will briefly review the significance of having living prophets. This will help remind us how important it is to listen and follow when the Brethren speak. We sustain the First Presidency and the Quorum of Twelve Apostles as "Prophets, Seers, and Revelators." Here, for a moment, we will look at the role of a "seer." The Prophet Joseph Smith emphasized this aspect of being a prophet when he taught the following about what ancient prophets "saw," including things in our day and things yet future for us (bold added for emphasis):

> "Wherefore, we again say, search the revelations of God; study the prophecies, and rejoice that God grants unto the world Seers and Prophets. They are they who saw the mysteries of godliness; they saw the flood before it came; they saw angels ascending and descending upon a ladder that reached from earth to heaven; they saw the stone cut out of the mountain, which filled the whole earth; they saw the Son of God come from the regions of bliss and dwell with men on earth; they saw the deliverer come out of Zion, and turn away ungodliness from Jacob; they saw the glory of the Lord when he showed the transfiguration of the earth on the mount; they saw every mountain laid low and every valley exalted when the Lord was taking vengeance upon the wicked; they saw truth spring out of the earth, and righteousness look down from heaven in the last days, before the Lord came the second time to gather his elect; they saw the end of wickedness on earth, and the Sabbath of creation crowned with peace; they saw the end of the glorious thousand years, when Satan was loosed for a little season; they saw the day of judgment when all men received according to their works, and they saw the heaven and the earth flee away to make room for the city of God, when the righteous receive an inheritance in eternity" (Joseph Smith, *Teachings of the Prophet Joseph Smith,* selected and arranged by Joseph Fielding Smith [Salt Lake City: Deseret Book Co., 1977], pages12-13).

In this quote from Joseph Smith, we are taught that prophets "see" the future. They "see" by the power of God and then tell us what they see. They are "watchmen on the tower," which is a scriptural phrase

3

referring to guards who stand high upon towers where they can "see" a long way off and warn the citizens of the city when danger is coming. Thus, our modern "prophets, seers, and revelators" have been, in effect, called of God to stand upon high "towers" and are given spiritual sight to "see" when danger is coming and to warn us of it. In **The Family: A Proclamation to the World**, they have strengthened us and warned us of coming dangers and of dangers which have already come among us.

It is interesting to go back in time to the days of the Prophet Joseph Smith and see the usage of words and vocabulary in his day, which could reflect his usage and meaning. One of the best sources for this is the 1828 edition of *The American Dictionary of the English Language* by Noah Webster, which has been reprinted and is also available in computer software programs such as "Gospel Link 2001," published by Deseret Book Company. In Webster's 1828 dictionary, the word "seer" is defined as follows: "A prophet; a person who foresees future events. I Sam. ix." In 1 Samuel 9:9, we read "(Beforetime in Israel, when a man went to enquire of God, thus he spake, Come, and let us go to the seer: for he that is now called a Prophet was beforetime called a Seer.)" This again emphasizes the importance of the role our modern prophets also have as "seers" as they guide and direct us and warn of dangers which they "see" as our "watchmen on the tower."

In August of 1990, I decided to go back about ten years to find specific examples of what our "seers" had seen coming. It was fascinating to find so many obvious examples of the "seership" of our First Presidency and Quorum of the Twelve. I will include here just a few examples of what I found.

Our society and culture is getting progressively more and more brutal and merciless. In the April 1990 General Conference, President Gordon B. Hinckley "saw" this and counseled, "We all need mercy." "Show more kindness to each other."

Sometimes, public activists and advocacy groups get out of balance. Because they fail to understand correct doctrine from God, they teach, either intentionally or due to lack of understanding, things which can be devastating to the divine nature of human beings. You have probably seen on television and read much in the newspapers about extreme animal rights activists who teach that animals, bugs, snails, owls, etc. are equal in importance to people. In their extremism, they push for laws which, in their ultimate effect, sometimes make people less important than other forms of life on earth. In fact, you have probably heard such activists proclaim that people themselves are merely more advanced animals. This can become very dangerous to our self-image as children of God, with the divine potential to become like Him. While we have a definite God-given responsibility to take care of our environment, we must keep proper perspective as to who we are and where we fit in. Have our "seers" seen the danger in such radicalism? Yes. For example, in the October 1990 General Conference of the Church, Elder Boyd K. Packer said,

> "When our youth are taught that they are but animals, they feel free, even compelled, to respond to every urge and impulse. We should not be so puzzled at what is happening to society."

By the way, are there any scriptures which actually say that mankind is more important than other creations of God? Answer: Yes. For instance, Matthew 6:26. We obviously must heed the strict charge from God to take good care of the whole ecology of our earth, but things can get tragically out of balance when misunderstanding or intentional deception takes over in public policy and law.

What have our "seers" seen with respect to gay and lesbian behavior? Answer:

> "We have seen the end of the road you are tempted to follow. It is not likely that a bishop can tell you what causes these conditions or why you are afflicted, nor can he erase the temptation. But he can tell you what is right and what is wrong. If you know right from wrong, you have a place to begin. That is the point at which individual choice becomes operative. That is the point at which repentance and forgiveness can exert great spiritual power. I believe that most people are drawn into a life of drug addiction or perversion or submit to an abortion without really realizing how morally and spiritually dangerous they are." (Elder Boyd K. Packer, October 1990 General Conference)

One of the great destructive battles in the last days is the battle over the equality of men and women. There have been countless tragic abuses based on the false idea that men are superior to women, but sometimes the battle to rectify the matter is more destructive and abusive than the issue itself. All fifteen of our modern "seers" (the First Presidency and the Quorum of the Twelve) have "seen" this and have given us the word of the Lord on this issue. What is it? Answer:

". . . fathers and mothers are obligated to help one another as equal partners." (The Family: A Proclamation to the World, September 23, 1995.)

The Church is growing at a wonderful and incredible rate. We are told by the Brethren that we must think in terms of 50 million members, of 100 million members, as we look to the future! Most organizations would be shaking in their boots at the prospects of keeping up with such tremendous growth. There would be long debates and much of concern as to how to cope with it.

But, what did President Hinckley "see" as our "Seer" with respect to this growth? In the October 1995 General Conference of the Church, he announced that he had "seen" D&C 107:98 with new eyes, that he had seen this verse as never before. In previous verses in section 107, the Lord had explained the organization and authority of the First Presidency (verses 21-22) that of the Twelve Apostles (verses 23-24, 33) the role and authority of the Seventy (verses 25-26, 34) the organization of deacons quorums (verse 85) teachers quorums (verse 86) priests quorums (verses 87-88) and elders quorums (verse 89). The Lord continued in verses 91-92 to explain that the President of the Church is "to be a seer, a revelator, a translator, and a prophet, having all the gifts of God which he bestows upon the head of the church." Then, in verses 93-97, we learn more about the role and responsibilities of the Seventy.

However, as President Hinckley pointed out, it seems that no one had previously paid much attention to verse 98. It is this:

> "Whereas other officers of the church, who belong not unto the Twelve, neither to the Seventy, are not under the responsibility to travel among all nations, but are to travel as their circumstances shall allow, notwithstanding they may hold as high and responsible offices in the church."

Upon reading this verse to the conference, President Hinckley announced the release of all 284 Regional Representatives, effective August 15, 1995, and went on to sustain Area Authority Seventies. These, he explained, are the "other officers" mentioned in D&C 107:98. And so, the Church growth is dealt with smoothly and effectively, under the direction of the Lord as these brethren serve throughout the world, often in area presidencies, and wherever their area presidencies need them to serve, including the calling of new stake presidents and the reorganization of stakes.

Speaking of growth, as a "seer" President Hinckley "saw" how to make temples available to far more members throughout the world. This resulted in the building of great numbers of smaller temples. In the October 1997 General Conference, President Hinckley announced the construction of these small temples as he said, "But there are many areas of the Church that are remote, where the membership is small and not likely to grow very much in the near future. Are those who live in these places to be denied forever the blessings of the temple ordinances? While visiting such an area a few months ago, we prayerfully pondered this question. The answer, we believe, came bright and clear. "We will construct small temples." You know the result of this revelation to the Lord's "seer." As of April 2003, there were a total of 114 temples in operation throughout the world.

The "Y-2K scare" (the worry among computer users as the year 2000 approached) was much publicized and much expense and time were consumed in preparing for the possibility that many computer systems would fail to adjust properly to the change from 1999 to 2000. The possibility of confusion and perhaps billions of dollars being lost because of computers not adjusting correctly to the thousand-year date change caused rightful concern. I had some concern myself as to whether or not my own computers would make the transition correctly. However, I took simple and peaceful comfort when I heard one of our "seers" speak out directly regarding the potential for world chaos as we switched from 1999 to 2000 in our computer-driven world. President James E. Faust in the April 1999 General Conference said, "While some glitches may occur, I am optimistic that no great catastrophic computer breakdown will disrupt society as we move into the next century." That was all I needed to hear.

More and more states and localities are legalizing gambling and lotteries. The Internet has many sites where people can gamble. Has God spoken through His "seers" on this issue? Absolutely! In the October 1999 General Conference, President Hinckley said, "We have opposed gambling and liquor and will continue to do so. We regard it as not only our right but our duty to oppose those forces which we feel undermine the moral fiber of society."

What do our "seers" see with respect to pornography? In many talks over many years, President Hinckley and others of the First Presidency and the Quorum of the Twelve have warned and forewarned members of the Church as well as all people everywhere against getting involved with pornography. They have "seen" the destruction that will come to individuals spiritually, emotionally, mentally, and in many cases, physically through involvement with this insidious evil.

And, what about the flood of sexual immorality in society? What about spouse and child abuse? What about failure to make family the top priority? What do the Brethren "see"? Answer: "We warn that individuals who violate covenants of chastity, who abuse spouse or offspring, or who fail to fulfill family responsibilities will one day stand accountable before God. Further, we warn that the disintegration of the family will bring upon individuals, communities, and nations the calamities foretold by ancient and modern prophets." (The Family: A Proclamation to the World, September 23, 1995.)

What about debt? What about "easy" credit? How many bank card offers do you receive almost weekly in the mail? What do our "Prophets, Seers, and Revelators" say about this? What is it that they "see" in our future if we get in over our heads because of unwise management of our financial resources? The answer is constant and consistent. In almost every general conference over the past several years as well as in focus articles in The Ensign and The Church News in recent years, the counsel has been to avoid unnecessary debt. The counsel has been to live "within" our financial means, which means to live "inside of" our income. In addition, the Brethren have counseled us to set aside some cash for emergencies, to live in housing which we can afford, and to have food storage on hand. The result of ignoring this counsel of our Seers is often devastating and tragic. Bankruptcies, stress, depression, and the breakup of marriages often have as their root cause the ignoring of the counsel of those who are appointed by the Lord to see into the future and warn us of coming problems while there is still time to make course corrections and avoid them.

And finally, since we live in a day and age when there is so much of despair and depression, of gloom and doom, what does our Prophet and Seer, President Gordon B. Hinckley, "see" with respect to this ever-worsening problem? How many times, especially over the last eight years since he became the President of the Church, have you heard him say, in one way or another, "What a great time to be alive!" "What a great time to be living!" This was a great help to me while I was serving as a stake president, because I occasionally had members approach me and express concern that our people were too happy, were laughing too much, telling too many funny jokes, etc. Their concern was that our members were acting as if they were unaware of the tragic suffering going on in the world, acting as if they were either naive or terribly insensitive to the misery of so many in this world. They felt that this behavior was wrong and that something should be done about it.

I appreciated their sensitivity, and while there is indeed much sorrow and suffering in the world, I was glad to have the vision of the living Prophet and used it to help open their understanding. About all I had to do was ask whether or not they had ever heard President Hinckley say, one way or another, "Be happy!" The answer was always, "Oh, yes, of course." And then a relaxed smile of understanding and relief would flow across their faces, as the significance of having such a direct answer to a deep concern enlightened their souls. Perhaps this is one of the most healing and significant things our "seers" help us to see, namely, that it is possible to be happy when surrounded by turmoil and evil.

With this in mind, we will turn our attention to current issues addressed by our First Presidency and the Council of the Twelve Apostles, who, as our "Seers" have told us in this marvelous document what they "see." For each issue we consider, we will show in bold type, in the proclamation, what the Brethren have said about it. Commentary in each chapter will be kept intentionally brief and simple in order to emphasize the power of the Proclamation itself.

A PROCLAMATION TO THE WORLD
THE FIRST PRESIDENCY AND COUNCIL OF THE TWELVE APOSTLES
OF THE CHURCH OF JESUS CHRIST OF LATTER-DAY SAINTS

We, the First Presidency and the council of the Twelve Apostles of The Church of Jesus Christ of Latter-day Saints, solemnly proclaim that marriage between a man and a woman is ordained of God and that the **family** is central to the Creator's plan for the eternal destiny of His children.

All human beings—male and female—are created in the image of God. Each is a beloved spirit son or daughter of heavenly parents, and, as such, each has a divine nature and destiny. Gender is an essential characteristic of individual premortal, mortal, and eternal identity and purpose.

In the premortal realm, spirit sons and daughters knew and worshiped God as their eternal Father and accepted His plan by which His children could obtain a physical body and gain earthly experience to progress toward perfection and ultimately realize his or her divine destiny as an heir of eternal life. The divine plan of happiness enables **family** relationships to be perpetuated beyond the grave. Sacred ordinances and covenants available in holy temples make it possible for individuals to return to the presence of God and for **families** to be united eternally.

The first commandment that God gave to Adam and Eve pertained to their potential for parenthood as husband and wife. We declare that God's commandment for His children to multiply and replenish the earth remains in force. We further declare that God has commanded that the sacred powers of procreation are to be employed only between man and woman, lawfully wedded as husband and wife.

We declare the means by which mortal life is created to be divinely appointed. We affirm the sanctity of life and of its importance in God's eternal plan.

Husband and wife have a solemn responsibility to love and care for each other and for their children. "Children are an heritage of the Lord." (Psalms 127:3.)

Parents have a sacred duty to rear their children in love and righteousness, to provide for their physical and spiritual needs, to teach them to love and serve one another, to observe the commandments of God and to be law-abiding citizens wherever they live. Husbands and wives—mothers and fathers—will be held accountable before God for the discharge of these obligations.

The **family** is ordained of God. Marriage between man and woman is essential to His eternal plan. Children are entitled to birth within the bonds of matrimony, and to be reared by a father and a mother who honor marital vows with complete fidelity. Happiness in **family** life is most likely to be achieved when founded upon the teachings of the Lord Jesus Christ. Successful marriages and **families** are established and maintained on principles of faith, prayer, repentance, forgiveness, respect, love, compassion, work, and wholesome recreational activities. By divine design, fathers are to preside over their **families** in love and righteousness and are responsible to provide the necessities of life and protection of their **families**. Mothers are primarily responsible for the nurture of their children. In these sacred responsibilities, fathers and mothers are obligated to help one another as equal partners. Disability, death, or other circumstances may necessitate individual adaptation. Extended **families** should lend support when needed.

We warn that individuals who violate covenants of chastity, who abuse spouse or offspring, or who fail to fulfill **family** responsibilities will one day stand accountable before God. Further, we warn that the disintegration of the **family** will bring upon individuals, communities, and nations the calamities foretold by ancient and modern prophets.

We call upon responsible citizens and officers of government everywhere to promote those measures designed to maintain and strengthen the **family** as the fundamental unit of society.

September 23, 1995

CHAPTER 3

THE FAMILY IS CENTRAL
TO THE FATHER'S PLAN FOR US

When you simply count the number of times the word "family" appears in the Proclamation in one form or another, and you find that it occurs thirteen times, the focus of this inspired document becomes clear. Family is indeed central to the Father's plan for us.

In the Proclamation (paragraph 2), we are reminded that we were members of a glorious family unit in premortality, and that we were deeply loved by our heavenly parents. We are accustomed to being members of a loving family. Our eternal worth and divine destiny, including our potential to become gods, was deeply ingrained in our hearts and minds there. In contrast, Satan and his evil hosts are doing everything they possibly can in our day to destroy the value of individuals including any concept of eternal destiny and worth.

In paragraph 3, the wording reminds us that the Father's plan is a plan of happiness. The highest happiness here in mortality, as well as in eternity, is found in living the gospel of Jesus Christ, and the gospel-centered family unit is the best place to learn this principle. It is interesting to note that although the doctrines and creeds of many religions do not teach that family units will exist in the next life, many, many people feel in their hearts that they will exist. The word of the Lord in this paragraph reinforces this feeling with the truth. Families can be united eternally, when members of families learn the truth, participate in sacred temple ordinances and thereafter keep the covenants they have made with God.

As you can see, many other aspects of the fundamental value of the family are mentioned in the proclamation. These will be dealt with separately later in this book.

A PROCLAMATION TO THE WORLD

THE FIRST PRESIDENCY AND COUNCIL OF THE TWELVE APOSTLES
OF THE CHURCH OF JESUS CHRIST OF LATTER-DAY SAINTS

We, the First Presidency and the council of the Twelve Apostles of The Church of Jesus Christ of Latter-day Saints, solemnly proclaim that **marriage** between a man and a woman is ordained of God and that the family is central to the Creator's plan for the eternal destiny of His children.

All human beings—male and female—are created in the image of God. Each is a beloved spirit son or daughter of heavenly parents, and, as such, each has a divine nature and destiny. Gender is an essential characteristic of individual premortal, mortal, and eternal identity and purpose.

In the premortal realm, spirit sons and daughters knew and worshiped God as their eternal Father and accepted His plan by which His children could obtain a physical body and gain earthly experience to progress toward perfection and ultimately realize his or her divine destiny as an heir of eternal life. The divine plan of happiness enables family relationships to be perpetuated beyond the grave. Sacred ordinances and covenants available in holy temples make it possible for individuals to return to the presence of God and for families to be united eternally.

The first commandment that God gave to Adam and Eve pertained to their potential for parenthood as husband and wife. We declare that God's commandment for His children to multiply and replenish the earth remains in force. We further declare that God has commanded that the sacred powers of procreation are to be employed only between man and woman, **lawfully wedded** as husband and wife.

We declare the means by which mortal life is created to be divinely appointed. We affirm the sanctity of life and of its importance in God's eternal plan.

Husband and wife have a solemn responsibility to love and care for each other and for their children. "Children are an heritage of the Lord." (Psalms 127:3.)

Parents have a sacred duty to rear their children in love and righteousness, to provide for their physical and spiritual needs, to teach them to love and serve one another, to observe the commandments of God and to be law-abiding citizens wherever they live. Husbands and wives—mothers and fathers—will be held accountable before God for the discharge of these obligations.

The family is ordained of God. **Marriage** between man and woman is essential to His eternal plan. Children are entitled to birth within the **bonds of matrimony**, and to be reared by a father and a mother who honor **marital vows** with complete fidelity. Happiness in family life is most likely to be achieved when founded upon the teachings of the Lord Jesus Christ. Successful **marriages** and families are established and maintained on principles of faith, prayer, repentance, forgiveness, respect, love, compassion, work, and wholesome recreational activities. By divine design, fathers are to preside over their families in love and righteousness and are responsible to provide the necessities of life and protection of their families. Mothers are primarily responsible for the nurture of their children. In these sacred responsibilities, fathers and mothers are obligated to help one another as equal partners. Disability, death, or other circumstances may necessitate individual adaptation. Extended families should lend support when needed.

We warn that individuals who violate covenants of chastity, who abuse spouse or offspring, or who fail to fulfill family responsibilities will one day stand accountable before God. Further, we warn that the disintegration of the family will bring upon individuals, communities, and nations the calamities foretold by ancient and modern prophets.

We call upon responsible citizens and officers of government everywhere to promote those measures designed to maintain and strengthen the family as the fundamental unit of society.

September 23, 1995

CHAPTER 4

THE INSTITUTION OF MARRIAGE IS GOD-GIVEN AND IS FUNDAMENTAL TO SOCIETY

Again, the inspired wording of the Proclamation emphasizes the word of the Lord against a very strong current trend in society, namely, the wide-spread acceptance of living together, including sexual intimacy, without being married. On the other hand, the Lord's word here serves to reinforce and support those who keep His commandments and who are determined to use the sacred powers of procreation only within the bonds of marriage. These clear and simple words provide a strong reminder to all the world that the commandments of God have not changed nor gone out of style.

Those who choose to live together in this worldly manner are indeed violating one of the Ten Commandments, namely, "Thou shalt not commit adultery." (Exodus 20:14) They are breaking the law of chastity. In Alma 39:5, Alma described this sin to his son, Corianton, in the following words:

> "Know ye not, my son, that these things are an abomination in the sight of the Lord; yea, most abominable above all sins save it be the shedding of innocent blood or denying the Holy Ghost?"

It appears that many members of the Church, young and old, are being caught up in the deception that, since so many are "doing it," it can't be that bad. Just because "everybody is doing it," the personal damage done to each individual is not lessened. Many years ago, in southeastern Utah, a herd of horses was driven out across a very narrow neck of rock onto the flat top of a high, small plateau. The men who drove the herd felt that they had a ready-made corral for the horses, since there was a sheer 1,000-foot dropoff all around the top of the plateau, except for the narrow path that led out onto it. All the men had to do was block the path so that it served as a corral gate. They did so. Their plan was to go out on the plateau, among the horses, choose the best ones, rope them and use them for riding stock. But, much to their astonishment and horror, the lead horse ran toward the edge and jumped over. All of the other horses followed. "Everybody did it." The fall of the last horse to go over was no less deadly than the fall of the lead horse. They all died. The large number of horses going over did not cancel the law of gravity, nor cancel the laws of inertia and momentum which governed the effects on each horse upon hitting the ground. This place is now known as Dead Horse Point State Park. The message is simple. Great numbers of people committing sin does not cancel God's commandments nor lessen the spiritual damage to each individual.

Another part of Satan's deception on this matter seems to be, "Since we have the technology nowadays to prevent conception, sleeping together as unmarrieds is no longer a concern." Such thinking promotes ignorance of the spiritual and emotional damage done to self and others. In fact, sexual immorality in any form is offensive to the Holy Ghost and can eventually lead to losing the Spirit as indicated in D&C 42:23, wherein the Lord says:

> "And he that looketh upon a woman to lust after her shall deny the faith, and shall not have the Spirit, and if he repents not he shall be cast out."

When we become insensitive to the Spirit, it makes us very vulnerable to the destructive forces of the devil. He then has much more power over us to destroy our happiness and peace and to make us unstable.

Thus, as is the case with other aspects of the Proclamation, the Lord is giving us counsel which promotes peace and stability right now in our lives as well as for eternity.

THE FAMILY

A PROCLAMATION TO THE WORLD

THE FIRST PRESIDENCY AND COUNCIL OF THE TWELVE APOSTLES
OF THE CHURCH OF JESUS CHRIST OF LATTER-DAY SAINTS

We, the First Presidency and the council of the Twelve Apostles of The Church of Jesus Christ of Latter-day Saints, solemnly proclaim that **marriage between a man and a woman** is ordained of God and that the **family is central** to the Creator's plan for the eternal destiny of His children.

All human beings—male and female—are created in the image of God. Each is a beloved spirit son or daughter of heavenly parents, and, as such, each has a divine nature and destiny. Gender is an essential characteristic of individual premortal, mortal, and eternal identity and purpose.

In the premortal realm, spirit sons and daughters knew and worshiped God as their eternal Father and accepted His plan by which His children could obtain a physical body and gain earthly experience to progress toward perfection and ultimately realize his or her divine destiny as an heir of eternal life. The divine plan of happiness enables family relationships to be perpetuated beyond the grave. Sacred ordinances and covenants available in holy temples make it possible for individuals to return to the presence of God and for families to be united eternally.

The first commandment that God gave to Adam and Eve pertained to their potential for parenthood as **husband and wife**. We declare that God's commandment for His children to multiply and replenish the earth remains in force. We further declare that God has commanded that the sacred powers of procreation are to be employed only between **man and woman**, lawfully wedded as **husband and wife**.

We declare the means by which mortal life is created to be divinely appointed. We affirm the sanctity of life and of its importance in God's eternal plan.

Husband and wife have a solemn responsibility to love and care for each other and for their children. "Children are an heritage of the Lord." (Psalms 127:3.)

Parents have a sacred duty to rear their children in love and righteousness, to provide for their physical and spiritual needs, to teach them to love and serve one another, to observe the commandments of God and to be law-abiding citizens wherever they live. **Husbands and wives—mothers and fathers—**will be held accountable before God for the discharge of these obligations.

The family is ordained of God. Marriage between man and woman is essential to His eternal plan. **Children are entitled to birth within the bonds of matrimony, and to be reared by a father and a mother** who honor marital vows with complete fidelity. Happiness in family life is most likely to be achieved when founded upon the teachings of the Lord Jesus Christ. Successful marriages and families are established and maintained on principles of faith, prayer, repentance, forgiveness, respect, love, compassion, work, and wholesome recreational activities. By divine design, **fathers** are to preside over their families in love and righteousness and are responsible to provide the necessities of life and protection of their families. **Mothers** are primarily responsible for the nurture of their children. In these sacred responsibilities, **fathers and mothers** are obligated to help one another as equal partners. Disability, death, or other circumstances may necessitate individual adaptation. Extended families should lend support when needed.

We warn that individuals who violate covenants of chastity, who abuse spouse or offspring, or who fail to fulfill family responsibilities will one day stand accountable before God. Further, we warn that the disintegration of the family will bring upon individuals, communities, and nations the calamities foretold by ancient and modern prophets.

We call upon responsible citizens and officers of government everywhere to promote those measures designed to maintain and strengthen the family as the fundamental unit of society.

September 23, 1995

CHAPTER 5

THE IMPORTANCE
OF THE TRADITIONAL FAMILY

Many in our current world are trying to redefine the family unit. On the national and international level, groups and individuals are lobbying on a very wide scale for agreements to change the definition of the family from the traditional two-parent family to the "anything goes" family. They are working with much power and momentum to legalize and legitimize in the public eye various "arrangements" in place of traditional families. These "arrangements" include having children out of wedlock, gay and lesbian couples adopting children or acquiring children through other means and technologies. This is all part of Satan's rather obvious and wide-open campaign to encourage sexual immorality, lack of commitment, infidelity, shirking of personal responsibility, and "me first" thinking.

As you can see, the word of the Lord in the Proclamation reaffirms the traditional family, consisting of a father, a mother, and children. As with other issues addressed in this inspired document, this very specific declaration goes against the grain of much modern thinking and teaching. Some members of the Church as well as many from other faiths who have dared to speak against these trends in large international conferences on the family have been ridiculed and scorned, even spit upon by disgusted delegates. Nevertheless, the word of the Lord is clear and if followed, points toward happiness and stability.

Again, the Proclamation encourages and reinforces those who choose to follow God's commandments and who make the traditional family the fundamental unit of society. It warns those who participate in redefining the traditional family that they are undermining society.

A PROCLAMATION TO THE WORLD

THE FIRST PRESIDENCY AND COUNCIL OF THE TWELVE APOSTLES
OF THE CHURCH OF JESUS CHRIST OF LATTER-DAY SAINTS

We, the First Presidency and the council of the Twelve Apostles of The Church of Jesus Christ of Latter-day Saints, solemnly proclaim that **marriage between a man and a woman** is ordained of God and that the family is central to the Creator's plan for the eternal destiny of His children.

All human beings—male and female—are created in the image of God. Each is a beloved spirit son or daughter of heavenly parents, and, as such, each has a divine nature and destiny. Gender is an essential characteristic of individual premortal, mortal, and eternal identity and purpose.

In the premortal realm, spirit sons and daughters knew and worshiped God as their eternal Father and accepted His plan by which His children could obtain a physical body and gain earthly experience to progress toward perfection and ultimately realize his or her divine destiny as an heir of eternal life. The divine plan of happiness enables family relationships to be perpetuated beyond the grave. Sacred ordinances and covenants available in holy temples make it possible for individuals to return to the presence of God and for families to be united eternally.

The first commandment that God gave to **Adam and Eve** pertained to their potential for parenthood **as husband and wife.** We declare that God's commandment for His children to multiply and replenish the earth remains in force. We further declare that God has commanded that **the sacred powers of procreation are to be employed only between man and woman, lawfully wedded as husband and wife.**

We declare the means by which mortal life is created to be divinely appointed. We affirm the sanctity of life and of its importance in God's eternal plan.

Husband and wife have a solemn responsibility to love and care for each other and for their children. "Children are an heritage of the Lord." (Psalms 127:3.)

Parents have a sacred duty to rear their children in love and righteousness, to provide for their physical and spiritual needs, to teach them to love and serve one another, to observe the commandments of God and to be law-abiding citizens wherever they live. Husbands and wives—mothers and fathers—will be held accountable before God for the discharge of these obligations.

The family is ordained of God. **Marriage between man and woman is essential to His eternal plan.** Children are entitled to birth within the bonds of matrimony, and to be reared by a father and a mother who honor marital vows with complete fidelity. Happiness in family life is most likely to be achieved when founded upon the teachings of the Lord Jesus Christ. Successful marriages and families are established and maintained on principles of faith, prayer, repentance, forgiveness, respect, love, compassion, work, and wholesome recreational activities. By divine design, fathers are to preside over their families in love and righteousness and are responsible to provide the necessities of life and protection of their families. Mothers are primarily responsible for the nurture of their children. In these sacred responsibilities, fathers and mothers are obligated to help one another as equal partners. Disability, death, or other circumstances may necessitate individual adaptation. Extended families should lend support when needed.

We warn that individuals who violate covenants of chastity, who abuse spouse or offspring, or who fail to fulfill family responsibilities will one day stand accountable before God. Further, we warn that the disintegration of the family will bring upon individuals, communities, and nations the calamities foretold by ancient and modern prophets.

We call upon responsible citizens and officers of government everywhere to promote those measures designed to maintain and strengthen the family as the fundamental unit of society.

September 23, 1995

CHAPTER 6

SAME SEX MARRIAGE

This is a very volatile and hotly-debated topic today. In a number of countries and even in a few states within the United States of America, same sex marriage has been legalized. The Church has been severely criticized for its stand against same sex marriage. The cry has gone forth for the Church and the Brethren to stay out of politics. Gay rights activists and many others have joined the attack, claiming that we as a church and as a people are bigoted and narrow-minded.

When people turn away from God and His commandments, they no longer see clearly.'In the fog of short-sightedness and the blindness of self-indulgence, they lose common sense. Indeed, wickedness does not promote rational thought. The Lord teaches us the value of commandments in D&C 59:4, wherein he says:

> "And they shall also be crowned with blessings from above, yea, and with commandments not a few, and with revelations in their time–they that are faithful and diligent before me."

Commandments are a blessing! They provide reference points for behavior, and for wise use of agency. They place us alongside of the "iron rod" which provides security, safety and stability. In verse four, quoted above, the Lord tells us that he will bless the faithful with many commandments and revelations. What a blessing the words of this proclamation are! In this case, they clearly state the commandment of the Lord with respect to same sex marriage.

Some people have even come to the conclusion that the Bible contains no commandments against same sex relationships. Some time ago, several students came to their institute of religion teacher very concerned because some students of religion on campus had told them that the Bible contains nothing against same sex relations. The teacher invited them to look in the Topical Guide of their LDS Bible, page 216, under Homosexuality, for a number of direct references to this topic. For example, in Romans 1:18, 26-27, the Apostle Paul says:

18 For the wrath of God is revealed from heaven against all ungodliness and unrighteousness . . .

26 . . . for even their women did change the natural use into that which is against nature: (lesbianism)

27 And likewise also the men, leaving the natural use of the woman, burned in their lust one toward another; men with men working that which is unseemly, (homosexuality)

Thus, the First Presidency and the Council of the Twelve Apostles have clearly and boldly reaffirmed the word of the Lord on this pervasive evil in our day. There can be no doubt left in the minds and hearts of faithful Latter-day Saints as to whether or not this is merely a matter of personal choice or an issue that strikes at the very foundations of society and human happiness.

A PROCLAMATION TO THE WORLD

THE FIRST PRESIDENCY AND COUNCIL OF THE TWELVE APOSTLES
OF THE CHURCH OF JESUS CHRIST OF LATTER-DAY SAINTS

We, the First Presidency and the council of the Twelve Apostles of The Church of Jesus Christ of Latter-day Saints, solemnly proclaim that marriage between a man and a woman is ordained of God and that the family is central to the Creator's plan for the eternal destiny of His children.

All human beings—male and female—are created in the image of God. Each is a beloved spirit son or daughter of heavenly parents, and, as such, each has a divine nature and destiny. Gender is an essential characteristic of individual premortal, mortal, and eternal identity and purpose.

In the premortal realm, spirit sons and daughters knew and worshiped God as their eternal Father and accepted His plan by which His children could obtain a physical body and gain earthly experience to progress toward perfection and ultimately realize **his or her divine destiny as an heir of eternal life.** The divine plan of happiness enables family relationships to be perpetuated beyond the grave. Sacred ordinances and covenants available in holy temples make it possible for individuals to return to the presence of God and for families to be united eternally.

The first commandment that God gave to Adam and Eve pertained to their potential for parenthood as husband and wife. We declare that God's commandment for His children to multiply and replenish the earth remains in force. We further declare that God has commanded that the sacred powers of procreation are to be employed only between man and woman, lawfully wedded as husband and wife.

We declare the means by which mortal life is created to be divinely appointed. We affirm the sanctity of life and of its importance in God's eternal plan.

Husband and wife have a solemn responsibility to love and care for each other and for their children. "Children are an heritage of the Lord." (Psalms 127:3.)

Parents have a sacred duty to rear their children in love and righteousness, to provide for their physical and spiritual needs, to teach them to love and serve one another, to observe the commandments of God and to be law-abiding citizens wherever they live. Husbands and wives—mothers and fathers—will be held accountable before God for the discharge of these obligations.

The family is ordained of God. Marriage between man and woman is essential to His eternal plan. Children are entitled to birth within the bonds of matrimony, and to be reared by a father and a mother who honor marital vows with complete fidelity. Happiness in family life is most likely to be achieved when founded upon the teachings of the Lord Jesus Christ. Successful marriages and families are established and maintained on principles of faith, prayer, repentance, forgiveness, respect, love, compassion, work, and wholesome recreational activities. By divine design, fathers are to preside over their families in love and righteousness and are responsible to provide the necessities of life and protection of their families. Mothers are primarily responsible for the nurture of their children. In these sacred responsibilities, fathers and mothers are obligated to help one another as equal partners. Disability, death, or other circumstances may necessitate individual adaptation. Extended families should lend support when needed.

We warn that individuals who violate covenants of chastity, who abuse spouse or offspring, or who fail to fulfill family responsibilities will one day stand accountable before God. Further, we warn that the disintegration of the family will bring upon individuals, communities, and nations the calamities foretold by ancient and modern prophets.

We call upon responsible citizens and officers of government everywhere to promote those measures designed to maintain and strengthen the family as the fundamental unit of society.

September 23, 1995

CHAPTER 7

THE WORTH OF EACH INDIVIDUAL
ON EARTH

In D&C 18:10, the Lord said:

"Remember the worth of souls is great in the sight of God."

One of the great truths of the gospel of Christ is that there was a premortal life and that all people are the offspring of God. The Bible teaches this very clearly. For instance, in Acts 17:28-29, we read the following (bold added for emphasis):

28 For in him we live, and move, and have our being; as certain also of your own poets have said, For **we are also his offspring**.

29 Forasmuch then as **we are the offspring of God**, we ought not to think that the Godhead is like unto gold, or silver, or stone, graven by art and man's device.

For whatever reasons, most Christian churches in our day do not teach that there was a premortal life, nor do they teach that we are literally children of God. They teach instead that we are God's creations and that there is no potential for our becoming remotely like Him. Additionally, some teach that very few will continue to live after this life. Believing such false doctrines can destroy the basic worth of each individual because it does away with the eternal nature of people. It does away with our worth as literal children of God. Imagine for a moment what it would do to your feelings of self-worth if you believed that you had no existence before this life and that it is highly likely that you will cease to exist after this life.

How refreshing it is to have modern prophets teach and reaffirm the true doctrine in this Proclamation. Each of us was a spirit child of heavenly parents in premortal life, and each of us has eternal purpose. Each has a divine destiny and will exist forever. Each has such worth that the Savior gave His life for us.

THE FAMILY

A PROCLAMATION TO THE WORLD

THE FIRST PRESIDENCY AND COUNCIL OF THE TWELVE APOSTLES
OF THE CHURCH OF JESUS CHRIST OF LATTER-DAY SAINTS

We, the First Presidency and the council of the Twelve Apostles of The Church of Jesus Christ of Latter-day Saints, solemnly proclaim that marriage between a man and a woman is ordained of God and that the family is central to the Creator's plan for the eternal destiny of His children.

All human beings—male and female—are created in the image of God. **Each is a beloved spirit son or daughter of heavenly parents**, and, as such, each has a divine nature and destiny. **Gender is an essential characteristic of individual premortal, mortal, and eternal identity and purpose.**

In the premortal realm, spirit sons and daughters knew and worshiped God as their eternal Father and accepted His plan by which His children could obtain a physical body and gain earthly experience to progress toward perfection and ultimately realize his or her divine destiny as an heir of eternal life. The divine plan of happiness enables family relationships to be perpetuated beyond the grave. Sacred ordinances and covenants available in holy temples make it possible for individuals to return to the presence of God and for families to be united eternally.

The first commandment that God gave to Adam and Eve pertained to their potential for parenthood as husband and wife. We declare that God's commandment for His children to multiply and replenish the earth remains in force. We further declare that God has commanded that the sacred powers of procreation are to be employed only between man and woman, lawfully wedded as husband and wife.

We declare the means by which mortal life is created to be divinely appointed. We affirm the sanctity of life and of its importance in God's eternal plan.

Husband and wife have a solemn responsibility to love and care for each other and for their children. "Children are an heritage of the Lord." (Psalms 127:3.)

Parents have a sacred duty to rear their children in love and righteousness, to provide for their physical and spiritual needs, to teach them to love and serve one another, to observe the commandments of God and to be law-abiding citizens wherever they live. Husbands and wives—mothers and fathers—will be held accountable before God for the discharge of these obligations.

The family is ordained of God. Marriage between man and woman is essential to His eternal plan. Children are entitled to birth within the bonds of matrimony, and to be reared by a father and a mother who honor marital vows with complete fidelity. Happiness in family life is most likely to be achieved when founded upon the teachings of the Lord Jesus Christ. Successful marriages and families are established and maintained on principles of faith, prayer, repentance, forgiveness, respect, love, compassion, work, and wholesome recreational activities. By divine design, fathers are to preside over their families in love and righteousness and are responsible to provide the necessities of life and protection of their families. Mothers are primarily responsible for the nurture of their children. In these sacred responsibilities, fathers and mothers are obligated to help one another as equal partners. Disability, death, or other circumstances may necessitate individual adaptation. Extended families should lend support when needed.

We warn that individuals who violate covenants of chastity, who abuse spouse or offspring, or who fail to fulfill family responsibilities will one day stand accountable before God. Further, we warn that the disintegration of the family will bring upon individuals, communities, and nations the calamities foretold by ancient and modern prophets.

We call upon responsible citizens and officers of government everywhere to promote those measures designed to maintain and strengthen the family as the fundamental unit of society.

September 23, 1995

CHAPTER 8

GENDER IS PART OF OUR ETERNAL IDENTITY

Gender differences, as part of the complimentary roles of men and women, add beauty to existence. Many of the deepest and purest emotions and feelings associated with human beings are a result of gender. Indeed, much of music, poetry, and prose as well as deepest thought has been inspired throughout history by the divinely given differences between women and men.

As is the case with other facets of joy and happiness here on earth, Satan is doing his evil utmost to pollute and confuse God's children on the matter of gender. Some feel dissatisfied with their gender. Some resort to surgical procedures in an attempt to change their gender. Scientists and philosophers enter into lengthy and often heated discussion on this topic. By ignoring God's word, they end up "Ever learning but never able to come to the knowledge of the truth." (2 Timothy 3:7)

As you can see, the truth here is found in God's word. It is given in clear, simple terms in "The Family: A Proclamation to the World." Our spirits have gender as taught in the phrase, "Each is a beloved spirit son or daughter of heavenly parents . . ." Many years ago, the First Presidency clearly taught that gender was part of our premortal existence when they said:

> "All men and women are in the similitude of the universal Father and Mother, and are literally the sons and daughters of Deity." (Joseph F. Smith, John R. Winder and Anthon H. Lund as quoted in James R. Clark's *Messages of the First Presidency of The Church of Jesus Christ of Latter-day Saints,* 4:203)

Gender will continue to be part of our identity forever. As taught in the Proclamation, "Gender is an essential characteristic of individual premortal, mortal, and eternal identity and purpose."

Some may argue that this approach is too simple and ignores realities which cause sorrow and suffering during mortality. Truth is the ultimate reality. Patience and faith are required in dealing with many aspects of this mortal probation. Concerns about gender-generated difficulties should not be made an exception to the gospel rules of faith and patience.

25

THE FAMILY

A PROCLAMATION TO THE WORLD

THE FIRST PRESIDENCY AND COUNCIL OF THE TWELVE APOSTLES
OF THE CHURCH OF JESUS CHRIST OF LATTER-DAY SAINTS

We, the First Presidency and the council of the Twelve Apostles of The Church of Jesus Christ of Latter-day Saints, solemnly proclaim that marriage between a man and a woman is ordained of God and that the family is central to the Creator's plan for the eternal destiny of His children.

All human beings—male and female—are created in the image of God. Each is a beloved spirit son or daughter of heavenly parents, and, as such, each has a divine nature and destiny. Gender is an essential characteristic of individual **premortal**, mortal, and eternal identity and purpose.

In the premortal realm, spirit sons and daughters knew and worshiped God as their eternal Father and accepted His plan by which His children could obtain a physical body and gain earthly experience to progress toward perfection and ultimately realize his or her divine destiny as an heir of eternal life. The divine plan of happiness enables family relationships to be perpetuated beyond the grave. Sacred ordinances and covenants available in holy temples make it possible for individuals to return to the presence of God and for families to be united eternally.

The first commandment that God gave to Adam and Eve pertained to their potential for parenthood as husband and wife. We declare that God's commandment for His children to multiply and replenish the earth remains in force. We further declare that God has commanded that the sacred powers of procreation are to be employed only between man and woman, lawfully wedded as husband and wife.

We declare the means by which mortal life is created to be divinely appointed. We affirm the sanctity of life and of its importance in God's eternal plan.

Husband and wife have a solemn responsibility to love and care for each other and for their children. "Children are an heritage of the Lord." (Psalms 127:3.)

Parents have a sacred duty to rear their children in love and righteousness, to provide for their physical and spiritual needs, to teach them to love and serve one another, to observe the commandments of God and to be law-abiding citizens wherever they live. Husbands and wives—mothers and fathers—will be held accountable before God for the discharge of these obligations.

The family is ordained of God. Marriage between man and woman is essential to His eternal plan. Children are entitled to birth within the bonds of matrimony, and to be reared by a father and a mother who honor marital vows with complete fidelity. Happiness in family life is most likely to be achieved when founded upon the teachings of the Lord Jesus Christ. Successful marriages and families are established and maintained on principles of faith, prayer, repentance, forgiveness, respect, love, compassion, work, and wholesome recreational activities. By divine design, fathers are to preside over their families in love and righteousness and are responsible to provide the necessities of life and protection of their families. Mothers are primarily responsible for the nurture of their children. In these sacred responsibilities, fathers and mothers are obligated to help one another as equal partners. Disability, death, or other circumstances may necessitate individual adaptation. Extended families should lend support when needed.

We warn that individuals who violate covenants of chastity, who abuse spouse or offspring, or who fail to fulfill family responsibilities will one day stand accountable before God. Further, we warn that the disintegration of the family will bring upon individuals, communities, and nations the calamities foretold by ancient and modern prophets.

We call upon responsible citizens and officers of government everywhere to promote those measures designed to maintain and strengthen the family as the fundamental unit of society.

September 23, 1995

CHAPTER 9

PREMORTAL EXISTENCE

In the Proclamation, the doctrine of a premortal existence is plainly taught and confirmed. As already mentioned in Chapter 7, the doctrine of a premortal existence is seldom, if ever, found in the formal teachings of Christian churches. It is interesting to note that the concept of a life prior to this life is indeed found in many non-Christian religions. Many members of those religions believe strongly that they lived on earth previously, perhaps as a person in a lower order of a caste system or whatever. This belief is often referred to as "reincarnation." While that belief is not correct—in Hebrews 9:27 we are taught that we only die once and will thereafter face judgment—it is nevertheless significant to observe that they essentially have more "truth" than their Christian counterparts, since they at least believe in some sort of life before this present one.

The Bible clearly teaches this essential truth. In Jeremiah 1:5 we read:

> "Before I formed thee in the belly I knew thee; and before thou camest forth out of the womb I sanctified thee, and I ordained thee a prophet unto the nations."

Hebrews 12:9 teaches that God is the Father of our spirits, thus indicating that we lived as spirits before we came to this earth:

> "Furthermore we have had fathers of our flesh which corrected us, and we gave them reverence: shall we not much rather be in subjection unto the Father of spirits, and live?"

In addition, D&C 93:29 teaches that our premortal intelligence (which continues to be an essential part of us) has existed forever. The Lord said:

> "Man was also in the beginning with God. Intelligence, or the light of truth, was not created or made, neither indeed can be."

Again, the Proclamation, given to all the world, clearly confirms the teaching of the Bible that all people lived in a premortal existence prior to entering into mortality. This simple truth gives meaning and perspective to mortal life, especially when it leads to the understanding in peoples' hearts that they personally and literally already know Heavenly Father.

Elder Boyd K. Packer taught how important it is to know that we had a premortal life when he said:

"There is no way to make sense out of life without a knowledge of the doctrine of premortal life.

"The idea that mortal birth is the beginning is preposterous. There is no way to explain life if you believe that. The notion that life ends with mortal death is ridiculous. There is no way to face life if you believe that.

"When we understand the doctrine of premortal life, then things fit together and make sense. We then know that little boys and little girls are not monkeys, nor are their parents, nor were theirs, to the very beginning generation.

"We are the children of God, created in his image.

"Our child-parent relationship to God is clear.

"The purpose for the creation of this earth is clear. The testing that comes in mortality is clear. The need for a redeemer is clear.

"When we do understand that principle of the gospel, we see a Heavenly Father and a Son; we see an atonement and a redemption.

"We understand why ordinances and covenants are necessary.

"We understand the necessity for baptism by immersion for the remission of sins. We understand why we renew that covenant by partaking of the sacrament" (Boyd K. Packer, in *Conference Report*, Oct. 1983, p. 22; or Ensign, Nov. 1983, p. 18).

THE FAMILY

A PROCLAMATION TO THE WORLD

THE FIRST PRESIDENCY AND COUNCIL OF THE TWELVE APOSTLES

OF THE CHURCH OF JESUS CHRIST OF LATTER-DAY SAINTS

We, the First Presidency and the council of the Twelve Apostles of The Church of Jesus Christ of Latter-day Saints, solemnly proclaim that marriage between a man and a woman is ordained of God and that the family is central to the Creator's plan for the eternal destiny of His children.

All human beings—male and female—are created in the image of God. Each is a beloved spirit son or daughter of heavenly parents, and, as such, each has a divine nature and destiny. Gender is an essential characteristic of individual premortal, mortal, and eternal identity and purpose.

In the premortal realm, spirit sons and daughters knew and worshiped God as their eternal Father and accepted His plan by which His children could obtain a physical body and gain earthly experience to progress toward perfection and ultimately realize his or her divine destiny as an heir of eternal life. **The divine plan of happiness** enables family relationships to be perpetuated beyond the grave. Sacred ordinances and covenants available in holy temples make it possible for individuals to return to the presence of God and for families to be united eternally.

The first commandment that God gave to Adam and Eve pertained to their potential for parenthood as husband and wife. We declare that God's commandment for His children to multiply and replenish the earth remains in force. We further declare that God has commanded that the sacred powers of procreation are to be employed only between man and woman, lawfully wedded as husband and wife.

We declare the means by which mortal life is created to be divinely appointed. We affirm the sanctity of life and of its importance in God's eternal plan.

Husband and wife have a solemn responsibility to love and care for each other and for their children. "Children are an heritage of the Lord." (Psalms 127:3.)

Parents have a sacred duty to rear their children in love and righteousness, to provide for their physical and spiritual needs, to teach them to love and serve one another, to observe the commandments of God and to be law-abiding citizens wherever they live. Husbands and wives—mothers and fathers—will be held accountable before God for the discharge of these obligations.

The family is ordained of God. Marriage between man and woman is essential to His eternal plan. Children are entitled to birth within the bonds of matrimony, and to be reared by a father and a mother who honor marital vows with complete fidelity. Happiness in family life is most likely to be achieved when founded upon the teachings of the Lord Jesus Christ. Successful marriages and families are established and maintained on principles of faith, prayer, repentance, forgiveness, respect, love, compassion, work, and wholesome recreational activities. By divine design, fathers are to preside over their families in love and righteousness and are responsible to provide the necessities of life and protection of their families. Mothers are primarily responsible for the nurture of their children. In these sacred responsibilities, fathers and mothers are obligated to help one another as equal partners. Disability, death, or other circumstances may necessitate individual adaptation. Extended families should lend support when needed.

We warn that individuals who violate covenants of chastity, who abuse spouse or offspring, or who fail to fulfill family responsibilities will one day stand accountable before God. Further, we warn that the disintegration of the family will bring upon individuals, communities, and nations the calamities foretold by ancient and modern prophets.

We call upon responsible citizens and officers of government everywhere to promote those measures designed to maintain and strengthen the family as the fundamental unit of society.

September 23, 1995

CHAPTER 10

WE HAD AGENCY AND ACCEPTED THE FATHER'S PLAN IN PREMORTALITY

One of the most important truths of all, which affects every aspect of our behavior, is the doctrine that we have moral agency. A companion doctrine is the fact that we are thus accountable for our actions. This gift of agency protects and preserves our individuality.

The Proclamation reaffirms that we were given agency in our premortal life and that we used it to accept the Father's plan for us. This "great plan of happiness" (Alma 42:8) brought tremendous joy to us there. Job 38:7 tells us that ". . . the morning stars sang together, and all the sons of God shouted for joy." (Note: the phrase "sons of God" is a generic term here which means "sons and daughters of God." See Job 38:7, footnote b, in our Bible.)

We understand from the scriptures that Satan sought to destroy God's spirit children in premortality "because of their agency." (D&C 29:36) It is important for us to understand that we did have agency there. This knowledge gives much additional meaning to our understanding of our premortal life. It means that we were growing, learning, and progressing toward our goal of becoming like our Father. It means that we were responsible for our decisions and resulting consequences there. It means that we have had eons of experience using moral agency already, before coming to this earth. It means that we are well-prepared to take our "final exam" on this "University of Earth."

Some might express concern that the veil, which was drawn across our memory of premortal life as we were born into mortality, does away with the value of premortal experience. Not so. While the veil takes away the memory of pre-earth life, it does not do away with our personality and the development and growth we experienced there. It comes through the veil with us. Indeed, Abraham 3:22-23 teaches us that "many of the noble and great ones" from premortality will become rulers and leaders in God's work here on earth. Abraham was one of these. In fact, D&C 93:38 teaches that the Father extended a great

THE PROCLAMATION ON THE FAMILY

blessing and kindness to each of us upon mortal birth. In this verse, the Lord explains that "Every spirit of man was innocent in the beginning;" (In other words, all of us started out innocent in our premortal life.) As we come to earth as infants, we are once again made "innocent before God." Then, through the Atonement of Christ, if we so desire, we can regain and maintain that purity and cleanness before God.

Here is the key point: The Proclamation teaches and confirms that agency is a vital component of our premortal and mortal individuality. Earth life is not the only time we have had moral agency. We were given it and used it to grow and progress or to stumble and fall in premortality. We were taught the gospel and the Father's plan there so that agency was meaningful. We joyfully accepted His plan for us. This knowledge gives us perspective here on earth. We know that this life is not the beginning of our interaction with God, rather that it is the continuation of life as children of the Father who have been sent away from home for our final schooling prior to "graduation" to exaltation or to "placement" into a lesser reward. Key elements leading up to final judgment are knowledge of the Father's plan, personal agency, and the Atonement of Christ.

A PROCLAMATION TO THE WORLD

THE FIRST PRESIDENCY AND COUNCIL OF THE TWELVE APOSTLES
OF THE CHURCH OF JESUS CHRIST OF LATTER-DAY SAINTS

We, the First Presidency and the council of the Twelve Apostles of The Church of Jesus Christ of Latter-day Saints, solemnly proclaim that marriage between a man and a woman is ordained of God and that the family is central to the Creator's plan for the eternal destiny of His children.

All human beings—male and female—are created in the image of God. Each is a beloved spirit son or daughter of heavenly parents, and, as such, **each has a divine nature and destiny.** Gender is an essential characteristic of individual premortal, mortal, and eternal identity and purpose.

In the premortal realm, spirit sons and daughters knew and worshiped God as their eternal Father and accepted His plan by which **His children could obtain a physical body and gain earthly experience to progress toward perfection and ultimately realize his or her divine destiny as an heir of eternal life.** The divine plan of happiness enables family relationships to be perpetuated beyond the grave. Sacred ordinances and covenants available in holy temples make it possible for individuals to return to the presence of God and for families to be united eternally.

The first commandment that God gave to Adam and Eve pertained to their potential for parenthood as husband and wife. We declare that God's commandment for His children to multiply and replenish the earth remains in force. We further declare that God has commanded that the sacred powers of procreation are to be employed only between man and woman, lawfully wedded as husband and wife.

We declare the means by which mortal life is created to be divinely appointed. We affirm the sanctity of life and of its importance in God's eternal plan.

Husband and wife have a solemn responsibility to love and care for each other and for their children. "Children are an heritage of the Lord." (Psalms 127:3.)

Parents have a sacred duty to rear their children in love and righteousness, to provide for their physical and spiritual needs, to teach them to love and serve one another, to observe the commandments of God and to be law-abiding citizens wherever they live. Husbands and wives—mothers and fathers—will be held accountable before God for the discharge of these obligations.

The family is ordained of God. Marriage between man and woman is essential to His eternal plan. Children are entitled to birth within the bonds of matrimony, and to be reared by a father and a mother who honor marital vows with complete fidelity. Happiness in family life is most likely to be achieved when founded upon the teachings of the Lord Jesus Christ. Successful marriages and families are established and maintained on principles of faith, prayer, repentance, forgiveness, respect, love, compassion, work, and wholesome recreational activities. By divine design, fathers are to preside over their families in love and righteousness and are responsible to provide the necessities of life and protection of their families. Mothers are primarily responsible for the nurture of their children. In these sacred responsibilities, fathers and mothers are obligated to help one another as equal partners. Disability, death, or other circumstances may necessitate individual adaptation. Extended families should lend support when needed.

We warn that individuals who violate covenants of chastity, who abuse spouse or offspring, or who fail to fulfill family responsibilities will one day stand accountable before God. Further, we warn that the disintegration of the family will bring upon individuals, communities, and nations the calamities foretold by ancient and modern prophets.

We call upon responsible citizens and officers of government everywhere to promote those measures designed to maintain and strengthen the family as the fundamental unit of society.

September 23, 1995

CHAPTER 11

PEOPLE CAN PROGRESS TO THE POINT OF BEING LIKE GOD

The phrase "eternal life" as used in the Proclamation occurs 99 times in the scriptures. It means "exaltation, becoming like God." You can turn to "Eternal Life" on page 125 of the Bible's Topical Guide and see that a synonym for eternal life is "exaltation." Exaltation is the type of life which the Father has. Compared to all other possible lifestyles given to people on judgment day, exaltation is "a far more, and an exceeding, and an eternal weight of glory." (See D&C 132:16 and 2 Corinthians 4:17.)

Romans 8:16 clearly tells us that "we are the children of God." Then in verse 17 the Apostle Paul plainly tells us that we are "heirs of God, and joint-heirs with Christ." How glorious, how encouraging, how enabling is the truth that we can become like God. What freedom it breathes to the human soul. What vision!

How different these truths are from the false teachings of Satan and his followers today. They seem to take delight in demeaning and destroying any idea of divine potential within us. They demote human life to the status of a biological accident, with neither an eternal past nor an eternal future, thus robbing God's children of any basic worth at all. Indeed, one of the most caustic ridicules heaped upon the Church and its members is the cry that we blaspheme God by teaching that we can become like Him. How tragic that such sweet scriptural truth should be destroyed in the angry flames of bigotry, leaving only intellectual ashes in their wake.

And again, the word of the Lord shines forth from the Proclamation with simple clarity, stating that each of us is capable of progressing "toward perfection" and that each of us can "realize his or her divine destiny as an heir of eternal life." We can become gods.

THE FAMILY
A PROCLAMATION TO THE WORLD
THE FIRST PRESIDENCY AND COUNCIL OF THE TWELVE APOSTLES
OF THE CHURCH OF JESUS CHRIST OF LATTER-DAY SAINTS

We, the First Presidency and the council of the Twelve Apostles of The Church of Jesus Christ of Latter-day Saints, solemnly proclaim that marriage between a man and a woman is ordained of God and that the family is central to the Creator's plan for the eternal destiny of His children.

All human beings—male and female—are created in the image of God. Each is a beloved spirit son or daughter of heavenly parents, and, as such, each has a divine nature and destiny. Gender is an essential characteristic of individual premortal, mortal, and eternal identity and purpose.

In the premortal realm, spirit sons and daughters knew and worshiped God as their eternal Father and accepted His plan by which His children could obtain a physical body and gain earthly experience to progress toward perfection and ultimately realize his or her divine destiny as an heir of eternal life. **The divine plan of happiness enables family relationships to be perpetuated beyond the grave.** Sacred ordinances and covenants available in holy temples make it possible for individuals to return to the presence of God and for **families to be united eternally.**

The first commandment that God gave to Adam and Eve pertained to their potential for parenthood as husband and wife. We declare that God's commandment for His children to multiply and replenish the earth remains in force. We further declare that God has commanded that the sacred powers of procreation are to be employed only between man and woman, lawfully wedded as husband and wife.

We declare the means by which mortal life is created to be divinely appointed. We affirm the sanctity of life and of its importance in God's eternal plan.

Husband and wife have a solemn responsibility to love and care for each other and for their children. "Children are an heritage of the Lord." (Psalms 127:3.)

Parents have a sacred duty to rear their children in love and righteousness, to provide for their physical and spiritual needs, to teach them to love and serve one another, to observe the commandments of God and to be law-abiding citizens wherever they live. Husbands and wives—mothers and fathers—will be held accountable before God for the discharge of these obligations.

The family is ordained of God. Marriage between man and woman is essential to His eternal plan. Children are entitled to birth within the bonds of matrimony, and to be reared by a father and a mother who honor marital vows with complete fidelity. Happiness in family life is most likely to be achieved when founded upon the teachings of the Lord Jesus Christ. Successful marriages and families are established and maintained on principles of faith, prayer, repentance, forgiveness, respect, love, compassion, work, and wholesome recreational activities. By divine design, fathers are to preside over their families in love and righteousness and are responsible to provide the necessities of life and protection of their families. Mothers are primarily responsible for the nurture of their children. In these sacred responsibilities, fathers and mothers are obligated to help one another as equal partners. Disability, death, or other circumstances may necessitate individual adaptation. Extended families should lend support when needed.

We warn that individuals who violate covenants of chastity, who abuse spouse or offspring, or who fail to fulfill family responsibilities will one day stand accountable before God. Further, we warn that the disintegration of the family will bring upon individuals, communities, and nations the calamities foretold by ancient and modern prophets.

We call upon responsible citizens and officers of government everywhere to promote those measures designed to maintain and strengthen the family as the fundamental unit of society.

September 23, 1995

CHAPTER 12

IT IS POSSIBLE FOR FAMILIES
TO BE TOGETHER ETERNALLY

Deep within each human heart, there seems to be a yearning for belonging. This is God-given and certainly has come through the veil with us. There are many things which the veil has not filtered out nor obscured, and this seems to be one of them. The feelings of belonging developed in caring, nurturing homes, seem to echo and reflect feelings developed in our heavenly home in premortality. They provide for stability here and enable giving of self in service to others. How wonderful that families can be together in the next life also!

Yet, how many Christian religions teach this as doctrine? Time and again, during my mission, as we taught the plan of salvation, emphasizing that families can be together forever, people would say, "I have always believed that, but my church says it is not true." This is one of the "plain and precious things" spoken of in 1 Nephi 13, which the adversary has taken away. Imagine being a member of a loving, caring family, but being taught that families are merely an earthly structure and association. Can you feel how that would cause conflict within your soul, wanting on the one hand to strengthen family bonds and ties, yet on the other hand feeling that it is an exercise in futility since such feelings and relationships die with death?

Modern prophets and apostles have clearly, sweetly stated the truth. It does away with feelings of futility. It encourages strong family ties and feelings, with the expectation that such bonds can last eternally.

THE FAMILY

A PROCLAMATION TO THE WORLD

THE FIRST PRESIDENCY AND COUNCIL OF THE TWELVE APOSTLES

OF THE CHURCH OF JESUS CHRIST OF LATTER-DAY SAINTS

We, the First Presidency and the council of the Twelve Apostles of The Church of Jesus Christ of Latter-day Saints, solemnly proclaim that marriage between a man and a woman is ordained of God and that the family is central to the Creator's plan for the eternal destiny of His children.

All human beings—male and female—are created in the image of God. Each is a beloved spirit son or daughter of heavenly parents, and, as such, each has a divine nature and destiny. Gender is an essential characteristic of individual premortal, mortal, and eternal identity and purpose.

In the premortal realm, spirit sons and daughters knew and worshiped God as their eternal Father and accepted His plan by which His children could obtain a physical body and gain earthly experience to progress toward perfection and ultimately realize his or her divine destiny as an heir of eternal life. The divine plan of happiness enables family relationships to be perpetuated beyond the grave. **Sacred ordinances and covenants available in holy temples make it possible for individuals to return to the presence of God and for families to be united eternally.**

The first commandment that God gave to Adam and Eve pertained to their potential for parenthood as husband and wife. We declare that God's commandment for His children to multiply and replenish the earth remains in force. We further declare that God has commanded that the sacred powers of procreation are to be employed only between man and woman, lawfully wedded as husband and wife.

We declare the means by which mortal life is created to be divinely appointed. We affirm the sanctity of life and of its importance in God's eternal plan.

Husband and wife have a solemn responsibility to love and care for each other and for their children. "Children are an heritage of the Lord." (Psalms 127:3.)

Parents have a sacred duty to rear their children in love and righteousness, to provide for their physical and spiritual needs, to teach them to love and serve one another, to observe the commandments of God and to be law-abiding citizens wherever they live. Husbands and wives—mothers and fathers—will be held accountable before God for the discharge of these obligations.

The family is ordained of God. Marriage between man and woman is essential to His eternal plan. Children are entitled to birth within the bonds of matrimony, and to be reared by a father and a mother who honor marital vows with complete fidelity. Happiness in family life is most likely to be achieved when founded upon the teachings of the Lord Jesus Christ. Successful marriages and families are established and maintained on principles of faith, prayer, repentance, forgiveness, respect, love, compassion, work, and wholesome recreational activities. By divine design, fathers are to preside over their families in love and righteousness and are responsible to provide the necessities of life and protection of their families. Mothers are primarily responsible for the nurture of their children. In these sacred responsibilities, fathers and mothers are obligated to help one another as equal partners. Disability, death, or other circumstances may necessitate individual adaptation. Extended families should lend support when needed.

We warn that individuals who violate covenants of chastity, who abuse spouse or offspring, or who fail to fulfill family responsibilities will one day stand accountable before God. Further, we warn that the disintegration of the family will bring upon individuals, communities, and nations the calamities foretold by ancient and modern prophets.

We call upon responsible citizens and officers of government everywhere to promote those measures designed to maintain and strengthen the family as the fundamental unit of society.

September 23, 1995

CHAPTER 13

THE SIGNIFICANCE OF TEMPLES AND ORDINANCES PERFORMED THERE

The word "ordinance" is used 57 times in the scriptures. "Ordinances" occurs 66 times. The word "covenant" is used 362 times. "Temple" is used 260 times. Most of the occurrences of these special words are found in the Bible. Yet, the majority of people who believe in God haven't the slightest idea how these words tie together.

Nephi of old was shown in vision that this would be the case.

> ". . . they have taken away from the gospel of the Lamb many parts which are plain and most precious; and also many covenants of the Lord have they taken away." (1 Nephi 13:26)

Additionally, Nephi was shown the tragic results that would follow this taking away.

> ". . . because of these things which are taken away out of the gospel of the Lamb, an exceedingly great many do stumble, yea, insomuch that Satan hath great power over them." (1 Nephi 13:29)

For many converts to the Church, one of the most appealing aspects of the true gospel as they first heard it preached was that of the temple and the fact that ordinances are performed therein, which bind us to God and seal families together forever.

One of the great values of each specific temple ordinance is that there is no doubt that you have made a specific covenant with God. There is nothing vague, foggy, hazy, or "iffy" about it. You know that you have participated in the ordinance and made specific covenants and that if you keep your part of the bargain, God is bound to keep His part (see D&C 82:10.) Therefore, you can plan on specific rewards and benefits now and in eternity.

Satan does his best to reduce Christ's gospel to vague generalities, thus eliminating specific hopes, commitments and expectations in religion. Into the midst of this spiritual blandness come the words of the modern Prophets and Apostles proclaiming that there are "sacred ordinances and covenants available in holy temples" today. The Proclamation is to all the world and these wonderful blessings are available to all who make themselves worthy!

A PROCLAMATION TO THE WORLD

THE FIRST PRESIDENCY AND COUNCIL OF THE TWELVE APOSTLES
OF THE CHURCH OF JESUS CHRIST OF LATTER-DAY SAINTS

We, the First Presidency and the council of the Twelve Apostles of The Church of Jesus Christ of Latter-day Saints, solemnly proclaim that marriage between a man and a woman is ordained of God and that the family is central to the Creator's plan for the eternal destiny of His children.

All human beings—male and female—are created in the image of God. Each is a beloved spirit son or daughter of heavenly parents, and, as such, each has a divine nature and destiny. Gender is an essential characteristic of individual premortal, mortal, and eternal identity and purpose.

In the premortal realm, spirit sons and daughters knew and worshiped God as their eternal Father and accepted His plan by which His children could obtain a physical body and gain earthly experience to progress toward perfection and ultimately realize his or her divine destiny as an heir of eternal life. The divine plan of happiness enables family relationships to be perpetuated beyond the grave. Sacred ordinances and covenants available in holy temples make it possible for individuals to return to the presence of God and for families to be united eternally.

The first commandment that God gave to Adam and Eve pertained to their potential for parenthood as husband and wife. We declare that God's commandment for His children to multiply and replenish the earth remains in force. We further declare that God has commanded that the sacred powers of procreation are to be employed only between man and woman, lawfully wedded as husband and wife.

We declare the means by which mortal life is created to be divinely appointed. We affirm the sanctity of life and of its importance in God's eternal plan.

Husband and wife have a solemn responsibility to love and care for each other and for their children. **"Children are an heritage of the Lord."** (Psalms 127:3.)

Parents have a sacred duty to rear their children in love and righteousness, to provide for their physical and spiritual needs, to teach them to love and serve one another, to observe the commandments of God and to be law-abiding citizens wherever they live. Husbands and wives—mothers and fathers—will be held accountable before God for the discharge of these obligations.

The family is ordained of God. Marriage between man and woman is essential to His eternal plan. Children are entitled to birth within the bonds of matrimony, and to be reared by a father and a mother who honor marital vows with complete fidelity. Happiness in family life is most likely to be achieved when founded upon the teachings of the Lord Jesus Christ. Successful marriages and families are established and maintained on principles of faith, prayer, repentance, forgiveness, respect, love, compassion, work, and wholesome recreational activities. By divine design, fathers are to preside over their families in love and righteousness and are responsible to provide the necessities of life and protection of their families. Mothers are primarily responsible for the nurture of their children. In these sacred responsibilities, fathers and mothers are obligated to help one another as equal partners. Disability, death, or other circumstances may necessitate individual adaptation. Extended families should lend support when needed.

We warn that individuals who violate covenants of chastity, who abuse spouse or offspring, or who fail to fulfill family responsibilities will one day stand accountable before God. Further, we warn that the disintegration of the family will bring upon individuals, communities, and nations the calamities foretold by ancient and modern prophets.

We call upon responsible citizens and officers of government everywhere to promote those measures designed to maintain and strengthen the family as the fundamental unit of society.

September 23, 1995

CHAPTER 14

ZERO GROWTH POPULATION

The term "zero growth population" refers to the philosophy held by many that the earth is overcrowded and not capable of supporting any more population growth. At first glance, this might seem to be a matter of personal preference or at worst, a demonstration of lack of wisdom. Some countries in which such thinking has prevailed in times past have found their population shrinking because of a low birthrate. This has led to a shrinking working population as older citizens retire and fewer younger people enter the work force. Tax burdens increase on those who work in order to support the needs of the elderly.

There is much more to it, however. Because of this belief, some nations have even passed laws restricting the number of children a couple may have to one or a maximum of two. The punishment for violating these laws is harsh, especially on the mother. Widespread abortion is a prominent byproduct of such restrictions. The widespread killing of newborn babies, especially females, is accepted and even encouraged in some cultures.

It seems that the farther societies depart from God's commandments and laws, the more likely they are to approve practices which would otherwise be abhorred. Wickedness does not promote rational thought. Many who would be held in check by righteous laws and by the sentiments of moral people find license to bully and be brutal under the guise of enforcing the laws of corrupt societies.

With respect to the capacity of the earth to support its people, the Lord said, "For the earth is full, and there is enough and to spare." (D&C 104:17) In light of this simple scriptural statement of fact, we come to the realization that the earth's capacity to sustain is not the problem. Rather, it is man's greed and mismanagement that is to blame.

The statement by the Brethren in this Proclamation that "God's commandment for His children to multiply and replenish the earth remains in force" is a bold statement of truth which, in many cases, flies in the face of public and private opinion. But many who have chosen intentionally not to have children or to unreasonably curtail births into their families are even now reaping the harvest of loneliness and lack of fulfillment warned of. Indeed, "Children are an heritage of the Lord." (Psalms 127:3) as quoted in this Proclamation.

One last note related to this matter. When topics arise such as family size, when to have children, and how many children to have, there is much misinformation given by well-meaning members of the Church. Past prophets are sometimes quoted rather than our current prophets (2003 A.D.), leading to confusion and sometimes contention.

We sing "We Thank Thee O God For a Prophet" but sometimes forget to listen to him. We extol "ongoing revelation" as a hallmark of the true church, yet fail to use it. In this matter of bringing children into the world, our current prophets and seers have basically counseled members that the matter of how many children to have and when to have them is a private matter between husband and wife and the Lord, and that members should not meddle in each other's lives on such matters. Members can ask their bishops to seek the counsel of the Brethren in instructions to them from Church leaders. This, coupled with the commandment to "multiply and replenish the earth" (Genesis 1:28) provides a principle-based foundation for joy in our posterity.

THE FAMILY

A PROCLAMATION TO THE WORLD

THE FIRST PRESIDENCY AND COUNCIL OF THE TWELVE APOSTLES
OF THE CHURCH OF JESUS CHRIST OF LATTER-DAY SAINTS

We, the First Presidency and the council of the Twelve Apostles of The Church of Jesus Christ of Latter-day Saints, solemnly proclaim that marriage between a man and a woman is ordained of God and that the family is central to the Creator's plan for the eternal destiny of His children.

All human beings—male and female—are created in the image of God. Each is a beloved spirit son or daughter of heavenly parents, and, as such, each has a divine nature and destiny. **Gender is an essential characteristic of individual premortal, mortal, and eternal identity and purpose.**

In the premortal realm, spirit sons and daughters knew and worshiped God as their eternal Father and accepted His plan by which His children could obtain a physical body and gain earthly experience to progress toward perfection and ultimately realize his or her divine destiny as an heir of eternal life. The divine plan of happiness enables family relationships to be perpetuated beyond the grave. Sacred ordinances and covenants available in holy temples make it possible for individuals to return to the presence of God and for families to be united eternally.

The first commandment that God gave to Adam and Eve pertained to their potential for parenthood as husband and wife. We declare that God's commandment for His children to multiply and replenish the earth remains in force. We further declare that God has commanded that **the sacred powers of procreation are to be employed only between man and woman, lawfully wedded as husband and wife.**

We declare **the means by which mortal life is created** to be **divinely appointed.** We affirm the sanctity of life and of its importance in God's eternal plan.

Husband and wife have a solemn responsibility to love and care for each other and for their children. "Children are an heritage of the Lord." (Psalms 127:3.)

Parents have a sacred duty to rear their children in love and righteousness, to provide for their physical and spiritual needs, to teach them to love and serve one another, to observe the commandments of God and to be law-abiding citizens wherever they live. Husbands and wives—mothers and fathers—will be held accountable before God for the discharge of these obligations.

The family is ordained of God. Marriage between man and woman is essential to His eternal plan. **Children are entitled to birth within the bonds of matrimony, and to be reared by a father and a mother who honor marital vows with complete fidelity.** Happiness in family life is most likely to be achieved when founded upon the teachings of the Lord Jesus Christ. Successful marriages and families are established and maintained on principles of faith, prayer, repentance, forgiveness, respect, love, compassion, work, and wholesome recreational activities. By divine design, fathers are to preside over their families in love and righteousness and are responsible to provide the necessities of life and protection of their families. Mothers are primarily responsible for the nurture of their children. In these sacred responsibilities, fathers and mothers are obligated to help one another as equal partners. Disability, death, or other circumstances may necessitate individual adaptation. Extended families should lend support when needed.

We warn that individuals who violate covenants of chastity, who abuse spouse or offspring, or who fail to fulfill family responsibilities **will one day stand accountable before God.** Further, we warn that the disintegration of the family will bring upon individuals, communities, and nations the calamities foretold by ancient and modern prophets.

We call upon responsible citizens and officers of government everywhere to promote those measures designed to maintain and strengthen the family as the fundamental unit of society.

September 23, 1995

CHAPTER 15

SEXUAL RELATIONSHIPS OUTSIDE OF MARRIAGE

First of all, it is important to note that the powers of procreation are God-given, clean, pure, and desirable. The Proclamation declares them to be "sacred" and "divinely appointed." This is simple, powerful doctrine and beautiful, comforting truth. Anything that is sacred and appointed by God is neither evil nor unclean by nature. Only through misuse does this power cause uncleanness and become a tool of the devil.

Again, it is very important that we realize that the powers of procreation are approved of and designed by God to play a central role in our happiness. In the *Encyclopedia of Mormonism* we read:

"The power of procreation is vital to the entire Plan of Salvation. It is held sacred, to be used 'only as the Lord has directed'; as such it is viewed as the 'very key' to happiness. (Encyclopedia of Mormonism, 1-4 vols., edited by Daniel H. Ludlow. New York: Macmillan, 1992, 856).

Elder Boyd K. Packer has taught:

"Within your body is the power to beget life, to share in creation. The only legitimate expression of that power is within the covenant of marriage. The worthy use of it is the very key to your happiness. Do not use the power prematurely, not with anyone. The misuse of it cannot be made right by making it popular" (Boyd K. Packer, Let Not Your Heart Be Troubled [Salt Lake City: Bookcraft, 1991].

The devil and those who support him are highly skilled at coming at issues from many different angles, including perverting truth in order to tempt and destroy souls. Among the many Satan-sponsored misconceptions about sex, we will note two in particular. First, he attempts to convince that the powers of procreation within us are natural (which is true); therefore, any use of them, at any time, with self or anyone else is perfectly justified (which is false). The Proclamation speaks very clearly against this destructive and wide-spread way of thinking.

Second, he seems to be quite successful in getting some who keep the law of chastity to consider these powers to be inherently evil or dirty, yet necessary for the bearing of children. The Proclamation clearly teaches that this is not true. Sadly, in either case, Lucifer often succeeds in polluting the sacred nature and intrinsic beauty of sex as a powerful bond between husband and wife in the marriage relationship.

In a world where we are constantly bombarded with media as well as private advocacy of "anything goes," including "wide open sex," it is vital that we heed the word of the Lord given and reiterated through "continuing revelation" in the Proclamation.

Finally, a student once asked in a seminary class, "Why should we save sex until marriage? After all, we have the technology now to prevent conception." A good question, sincerely asked. The answer is important and includes the word of the Lord in D&C 42:23, wherein He says, "He that looketh upon a woman to lust after her shall deny the faith, and shall not have the Spirit." The possibility of pregnancy is not the only reason to abstain from illicit sex. Sexual immorality is offensive to the Spirit, and with continued involvement in such sin, individuals lose their sensitivity to the Holy Ghost. The Spirit is eventually withdrawn, and the person becomes very vulnerable to the devil. In addition, there are emotional and psychological penalties, including low self-esteem, insecurity and terrible loneliness. Gratefully, through deep and sincere repentance, the Atonement of Christ can restore moral cleanliness and the Spirit can return.

A PROCLAMATION TO THE WORLD
THE FIRST PRESIDENCY AND COUNCIL OF THE TWELVE APOSTLES
OF THE CHURCH OF JESUS CHRIST OF LATTER-DAY SAINTS

We, the First Presidency and the council of the Twelve Apostles of The Church of Jesus Christ of Latter-day Saints, solemnly proclaim that marriage between a man and a woman is ordained of God and that the family is central to the Creator's plan for the eternal destiny of His children.

All human beings—male and female—are created in the image of God. Each is a beloved spirit son or daughter of heavenly parents, and, as such, **each has a divine nature and destiny.** Gender is an essential characteristic of individual premortal, mortal, and eternal identity and purpose.

In the premortal realm, spirit sons and daughters knew and worshiped God as their eternal Father and accepted His plan by which His children could obtain a physical body and gain earthly experience to progress toward perfection and ultimately realize his or her divine destiny as an heir of eternal life. The divine plan of happiness enables family relationships to be perpetuated beyond the grave. Sacred ordinances and covenants available in holy temples make it possible for individuals to return to the presence of God and for families to be united eternally.

The first commandment that God gave to Adam and Eve pertained to their potential for parenthood as husband and wife. We declare that God's commandment for His children to multiply and replenish the earth remains in force. We further declare that God has commanded that the sacred powers of procreation are to be employed only between man and woman, lawfully wedded as husband and wife.

We declare the means by which mortal life is created to be divinely appointed. **We affirm the sanctity of life and of its importance in God's eternal plan.**

Husband and wife have a solemn responsibility to love and care for each other and for their children. "Children are an heritage of the Lord." (Psalms 127:3.)

Parents have a sacred duty to rear their children in love and righteousness, to provide for their physical and spiritual needs, to teach them to love and serve one another, to observe the commandments of God and to be law-abiding citizens wherever they live. Husbands and wives—mothers and fathers—will be held accountable before God for the discharge of these obligations.

The family is ordained of God. Marriage between man and woman is essential to His eternal plan. Children are entitled to birth within the bonds of matrimony, and to be reared by a father and a mother who honor marital vows with complete fidelity. Happiness in family life is most likely to be achieved when founded upon the teachings of the Lord Jesus Christ. Successful marriages and families are established and maintained on principles of faith, prayer, repentance, forgiveness, respect, love, compassion, work, and wholesome recreational activities. By divine design, fathers are to preside over their families in love and righteousness and are responsible to provide the necessities of life and protection of their families. Mothers are primarily responsible for the nurture of their children. In these sacred responsibilities, fathers and mothers are obligated to help one another as equal partners. Disability, death, or other circumstances may necessitate individual adaptation. Extended families should lend support when needed.

We warn that individuals who violate covenants of chastity, who abuse spouse or offspring, or who fail to fulfill family responsibilities will one day stand accountable before God. Further, we warn that the disintegration of the family will bring upon individuals, communities, and nations the calamities foretold by ancient and modern prophets.

We call upon responsible citizens and officers of government everywhere to promote those measures designed to maintain and strengthen the family as the fundamental unit of society.

September 23, 1995

CHAPTER 16

THE SANCTITY OF LIFE: ABORTION, EUTHANASIA (MERCY KILLING), SUICIDE

"Each has a divine nature and destiny." and "We affirm the sanctity of life." Simple, clear statements of doctrine. Each individual has infinite value and worth. God has divine stewardship over life and death. Yet, a great many people unthinkingly or intentionally take upon themselves the role of God in promoting abortion on demand, mercy killing, assisted suicide etc.

We must be careful as we deal with these matters, because, for instance, Church leaders have said that abortion may be necessary in some cases of rape, incest, or when the life of the mother is in jeopardy. Also, the Brethren have counseled that prolonging life by machines beyond reasonable means is unnecessary. In each case, members are counseled to seek the will of the Lord and to counsel with their local leaders of the Church when such decisions have to be faced.

Abortion on demand is very widespread as a means of birth control. It flies directly in the face of the "sanctity of life" as reaffirmed in the Proclamation. Even late-term abortion is supported by majority public opinion and by law in many nations and localities. The easy availability of abortion often goes hand-in-hand with sexual immorality. As is often the case, Satan combines one form of sin in an unholy alliance with another. Each unborn child has "a divine nature and destiny." Each life is sacred. We consider life to be sacred from the point of conception.

Euthanasia or "mercy killing" as it is more commonly called, is gaining status and momentum in public opinion as a means of terminating life. It also shows up now as "assisted suicide." The suffering associated with terminal illness and disease is often heart-rending and very difficult, and without an eternal perspective it often becomes impossible to understand. Many well-meaning people fail to see any purpose in such suffering, and thus advocate mercy killing.

One day, my father, who was terminally ill with cancer, having been bedridden for many months, motioned for me to come close where I could hear his strained whisper. We had just given him a blessing in which we had asked the Lord to let him pass on as soon as harmony with His will would permit. I knelt by his bedside as he whispered, "Dave, I don't want to die until I have learned all that the Lord wants me to learn from this life." I learned a most valuable lesson right there—one that is written permanently in my mind and on my heart. I believe I now better understand the Lord's counsel to the Prophet Joseph Smith in Liberty Jail when He said, "And then, if thou endure it well, God shall exalt thee on high; thou shalt triumph over all thy foes." (D&C 121:8) Dad was determined to "endure it well," to "triumph," to learn any lessons remaining in God's wisdom for him.

My observation is that there are many lessons for people to learn, both for the sufferers and for those who minister to them. Such lessons and character development are likewise "terminated" when life is terminated prematurely by so-called mercy killing.

Suicide is also a sensitive subject. The "sanctity of life" principle taught in the Proclamation applies here, too. Again, the length of our lives should be left in the hands of God. Taking one's own life can eliminate potential growth, which can come through dealing with setbacks and adversity. Committing suicide can leave life-long heartache, anguish, and unanswered questions in the hearts and souls of loved ones left behind. Suicide can thus, under most circumstances, be a highly selfish act.

Many ask, "What is the status of those who commit suicide?" "Is it murder if they take their own lives?" "Can they be forgiven?" "If they are endowed, can they be buried in their temple clothes?" We understand that each case of suicide will be judged individually and completely fairly by the Lord, based on the individual circum-stances. Thus, some will still have the option in the next life to progress on to exaltation. Others will go into other kingdoms of glory. And yes, those who were endowed can be buried in their temple clothes, provided that they had not lost their membership in the Church through excommunication before death. We are not judges. Thankfully, the Lord is the final judge.

THE FAMILY

A PROCLAMATION TO THE WORLD

THE FIRST PRESIDENCY AND COUNCIL OF THE TWELVE APOSTLES
OF THE CHURCH OF JESUS CHRIST OF LATTER-DAY SAINTS

We, the First Presidency and the council of the Twelve Apostles of The Church of Jesus Christ of Latter-day Saints, solemnly proclaim that marriage between a man and a woman is ordained of God and that the family is central to the Creator's plan for the eternal destiny of His children.

All human beings—male and female—are created in the image of God. Each is a beloved spirit son or daughter of heavenly parents, and, as such, each has a divine nature and destiny. Gender is an essential characteristic of individual premortal, mortal, and eternal identity and purpose.

In the premortal realm, spirit sons and daughters knew and worshiped God as their eternal Father and accepted His plan by which His children could obtain a physical body and gain earthly experience to progress toward perfection and ultimately realize his or her divine destiny as an heir of eternal life. The divine plan of happiness enables family relationships to be perpetuated beyond the grave. Sacred ordinances and covenants available in holy temples make it possible for individuals to return to the presence of God and for families to be united eternally.

The first commandment that God gave to Adam and Eve pertained to their potential for parenthood as husband and wife. We declare that God's commandment for His children to multiply and replenish the earth remains in force. We further declare that God has commanded that the sacred powers of procreation are to be employed only between man and woman, lawfully wedded as husband and wife.

We declare the means by which mortal life is created to be divinely appointed. We affirm the sanctity of life and of its importance in God's eternal plan.

Husband and wife have a solemn responsibility to love and care for each other and for their children. "Children are an heritage of the Lord." (Psalms 127:3.)

Parents have a **sacred duty** to rear their children in love and righteousness, to **provide** for their physical and spiritual needs, to **teach** them to love and serve one another, to observe the commandments of God and to be law-abiding citizens wherever they live. Husbands and wives—mothers and fathers—will be **held accountable before God** for the discharge of these **obligations**.

The family is ordained of God. Marriage between man and woman is essential to His eternal plan. Children are entitled to birth within the bonds of matrimony, and to be reared by a father and a mother who honor marital vows with complete fidelity. Happiness in family life is most likely to be achieved when founded upon the teachings of the Lord Jesus Christ. Successful marriages and families are established and maintained on principles of faith, prayer, repentance, forgiveness, respect, love, compassion, work, and wholesome recreational activities. By divine design, fathers are to preside over their families in love and righteousness and are responsible to provide the necessities of life and protection of their families. Mothers are primarily responsible for the nurture of their children. In these sacred responsibilities, fathers and mothers are obligated to help one another as equal partners. Disability, death, or other circumstances may necessitate individual adaptation. Extended families should lend support when needed.

We warn that individuals who violate covenants of chastity, who abuse spouse or offspring, or who fail to fulfill family responsibilities will one day stand accountable before God. Further, we warn that the disintegration of the family will bring upon individuals, communities, and nations the calamities foretold by ancient and modern prophets.

We call upon responsible citizens and officers of government everywhere to promote those measures designed to maintain and strengthen the family as the fundamental unit of society.

September 23, 1995

CHAPTER 17

THE SERIOUSNESS
OF MARRIAGE RESPONSIBILITIES

Just looking at the highlighted words in the copy of the Proclamation that goes with this chapter, one gets an idea of the seriousness of the commitments which go with marriage. Commitment to worthy causes brings stability, satisfaction, and meaning to the life of each individual who is willing to make such dedication a part of his or her being.

It is said that the Lord wanted to put each of us into a laboratory environment here on "The University of Earth" in which we could experience maximum character growth and development toward becoming like Him. He chose the family unit as the ideal "lab" for us. As with other success-producing "lab" experiences in actual colleges and universities, this lab requires commitment. The Proclamation reminds us of this with such words as "solemn responsibility," "love," "care for," "sacred duty," "provide for," "teach," "held accountable before God," and "obligations."

No wonder the Adversary is doing so much to cheapen and eliminate the power of personal commitment as it relates to the family as the basic unit of society. It is sad to note that as commitment to spouse, children, and extended family erode, so also does commitment to community, employer, and country. Selfishness, greed, and "me first" couched in such catch phrases as "self-actualization" become the main focus of existence and thus destroy the very foundations of humanity.

By following the counsel of the Lord on this matter, as re-emphasized in the Proclamation, each of us has the opportunity to examine and come to better understand the immediate as well as eternal value of commitment to righteous causes. The family is indeed the best "lab" for developing the Christlike qualities of dedication, loyalty, and commitment. Each individual benefits. All of society benefits. Much higher levels of personal joy, happiness, and satisfaction await those who catch the vision and import of this counsel and act upon it. The rewards of making family top priority are immediate as well as eternal. Even the father of the prodigal son (Luke 15), in spite of the daily magnification of heartache which dedication to his rebellious and foolish son caused, developed a higher quality of compassion that flowered fully upon the return of his much-missed and much-loved son.

One needs but to look at the trends in our current society to readily see that they go counter to what is best for us individually and collectively. Many do not even make the commitment of marriage. They want to "try things out first." Or, they simply do not want to be tied down to any long term commitments or legal liabilities of any type.

On a larger scale, many enter into legal agreements in business or in private ventures with no intention of keeping their part of the bargain unless the arrangement continues to satisfy their own desires. If and when things are no longer satisfactory to them, they simply hire a lawyer to get them out of the situation.

As you have no doubt observed by now, every item of counsel and direction given by the Lord in the Proclamation is designed by Him to benefit society as a whole as well as us individually in our quest for Exaltation, both here on earth as well as eternally. One does not need to wait for the next life for a clear conscience, nor for the personal growth and satisfaction which come with adhering to the Lord's "great plan of happiness." (Alma 42:8) In fact, if society as a whole ceases to be based on God-given principles, individual freedom is soon destroyed and Satan's goals are furthered.

Thus, the commitments inherent in proper marriage are fundamental to the survival of society and to individual freedom and growth.

A PROCLAMATION TO THE WORLD

THE FIRST PRESIDENCY AND COUNCIL OF THE TWELVE APOSTLES
OF THE CHURCH OF JESUS CHRIST OF LATTER-DAY SAINTS

We, the First Presidency and the council of the Twelve Apostles of The Church of Jesus Christ of Latter-day Saints, solemnly proclaim that marriage between a man and a woman is ordained of God and that **the family is central to the Creator's plan for the eternal destiny of His children.**

All human beings—male and female—are created in the image of God. Each is a beloved spirit son or daughter of heavenly parents, and, as such, each has a divine nature and destiny. Gender is an essential characteristic of individual premortal, mortal, and eternal identity and purpose.

In the premortal realm, spirit sons and daughters knew and worshiped God as their eternal Father and accepted His plan by which His children could obtain a physical body and gain earthly experience to progress toward perfection and ultimately realize his or her divine destiny as an heir of eternal life. The divine plan of happiness enables family relationships to be perpetuated beyond the grave. Sacred ordinances and covenants available in holy temples make it possible for individuals to return to the presence of God and for families to be united eternally.

The first commandment that God gave to Adam and Eve pertained to their potential for parenthood as husband and wife. We declare that **God's commandment for His children to multiply and replenish the earth remains in force.** We further declare that God has commanded that the sacred powers of procreation are to be employed only between man and woman, lawfully wedded as husband and wife.

We declare the means by which mortal life is created to be divinely appointed. We affirm the sanctity of life and of its importance in God's eternal plan.

Husband and wife have a solemn responsibility to love and care for each other and for their children. **"Children are an heritage of the Lord."** (Psalms 127:3.)

Parents have a sacred duty to rear their children in love and righteousness, to provide for their physical and spiritual needs, to teach them to love and serve one another, to observe the commandments of God and to be law-abiding citizens wherever they live. Husbands and wives—mothers and fathers—will be held accountable before God for the discharge of these obligations.

The family is ordained of God. Marriage between man and woman is essential to His eternal plan. Children are entitled to birth within the bonds of matrimony, and to be reared by a father and a mother who honor marital vows with complete fidelity. Happiness in family life is most likely to be achieved when founded upon the teachings of the Lord Jesus Christ. Successful marriages and families are established and maintained on principles of faith, prayer, repentance, forgiveness, respect, love, compassion, work, and wholesome recreational activities. By divine design, fathers are to preside over their families in love and righteousness and are responsible to provide the necessities of life and protection of their families. Mothers are primarily responsible for the nurture of their children. In these sacred responsibilities, fathers and mothers are obligated to help one another as equal partners. Disability, death, or other circumstances may necessitate individual adaptation. Extended families should lend support when needed.

We warn that individuals who violate covenants of chastity, who abuse spouse or offspring, or who fail to fulfill family responsibilities will one day stand accountable before God. Further, we warn that the disintegration of the family will bring upon individuals, communities, and nations the calamities foretold by ancient and modern prophets.

We call upon responsible citizens and officers of government everywhere to promote those measures designed to maintain and strengthen the family as the fundamental unit of society.

September 23, 1995

CHAPTER 18

THE IMPORTANCE OF HAVING CHILDREN

From a purely doctrinal, factual standpoint, the necessity of our having children is obvious. The myriads of spirit children of our Heavenly Parents have but one way to obtain physical bodies, namely, mortal birth. We all "shouted for joy" (Job 38:7) in the premortal council as we were told that our opportunity to come to earth was in place. By our choosing parenthood as married couples, we unselfishly open the doors for our spirit brothers and sisters to receive the great, eternal gift of a physical body.

While there is much more to it than providing a physical body and welcoming each spirit into a home, that gift itself is no small matter. Each mother goes "through the valley of the shadow of death" (Psalms 23:4) in order to bring forth a child, and each father makes a long-term commitment to work and provide the daily necessities of life. Both parents subjugate many of their own needs and desires for the good of their children. The words of the Lord in the Proclamation sustain such righteous choices on the part of parents in the face of much contrary philosophy and sentiment from the world at large.

To many, the having of children seems like the condemning of ones self to a dismal future of servitude and drudgery. Many voices in the secular world agree. The scriptures disagree.

> "As arrows are in the hand of a mighty man; so are children of the youth. Happy is the man that hath his quiver full of them." (Psalms 127:4-5)

Many of you no doubt are acquainted with individuals, now advancing in years, who have chosen not to have children. Not only have they intentionally denied themselves the deep joys and satisfactions—along with personal growth and development through the years—which attend rearing of children, but now, in their declining years, they find themselves bitterly lonely. The bitterness which accompanies the results of deliberate, selfish choices is far darker than otherwise.

59

In D&C 59:4, the Lord gives us a vital perspective about His commandments. They are designed to lead us to joy and happiness. He said, speaking of His faithful saints,

"And they shall also be crowned with blessings from above, yea, and with commandments not a few."

The Lord "blessed" Adam and Eve with the commandment to "multiply and replenish the earth." (Genesis 128) We too can be so blessed. Satan takes great satisfaction in twisting peoples' perspective such that they view God's commandments as unreasonable and unnecessary limitations on individual freedom. Such is the view of many who advocate not having children. For such, the harvest of discontent and loneliness is sure. Heeding the Proclamation could spare them this misery.

For those who desire marriage and posterity but are denied the joys of having children in this life, there is comfort in the fact that in the eternities, through their faithfulness here, they will have all the blessings and satisfactions of parenthood.

A PROCLAMATION TO THE WORLD
THE FIRST PRESIDENCY AND COUNCIL OF THE TWELVE APOSTLES
OF THE CHURCH OF JESUS CHRIST OF LATTER-DAY SAINTS

We, the First Presidency and the council of the Twelve Apostles of The Church of Jesus Christ of Latter-day Saints, solemnly proclaim that marriage between a man and a woman is ordained of God and that the family is central to the Creator's plan for the eternal destiny of His children.

All human beings—male and female—are created in the image of God. Each is a beloved spirit son or daughter of heavenly parents, and, as such, each has a divine nature and destiny. Gender is an essential characteristic of individual premortal, mortal, and eternal identity and purpose.

In the premortal realm, spirit sons and daughters knew and worshiped God as their eternal Father and accepted His plan by which His children could obtain a physical body and gain earthly experience to progress toward perfection and ultimately realize his or her divine destiny as an heir of eternal life. The divine plan of happiness enables family relationships to be perpetuated beyond the grave. Sacred ordinances and covenants available in holy temples make it possible for individuals to return to the presence of God and for families to be united eternally.

The first commandment that God gave to Adam and Eve pertained to their potential for parenthood as husband and wife. We declare that God's commandment for His children to multiply and replenish the earth remains in force. We further declare that God has commanded that the sacred powers of procreation are to be employed only between man and woman, lawfully wedded as husband and wife.

We declare the means by which mortal life is created to be divinely appointed. We affirm the sanctity of life and of its importance in God's eternal plan.

Husband and wife have a solemn responsibility to love and care for each other and for their children. "Children are an heritage of the Lord." (Psalms 127:3.)

Parents have a sacred duty to rear their children in love and righteousness, to provide for their physical and spiritual needs, to teach them to love and serve one another, to observe the commandments of God and to **be law-abiding citizens wherever they live.** Husbands and wives—mothers and fathers—will be held accountable before God for the discharge of these obligations.

The family is ordained of God. Marriage between man and woman is essential to His eternal plan. Children are entitled to birth within the bonds of matrimony, and to be reared by a father and a mother who honor marital vows with complete fidelity. Happiness in family life is most likely to be achieved when founded upon the teachings of the Lord Jesus Christ. Successful marriages and families are established and maintained on principles of faith, prayer, repentance, forgiveness, respect, love, compassion, work, and wholesome recreational activities. By divine design, fathers are to preside over their families in love and righteousness and are responsible to provide the necessities of life and protection of their families. Mothers are primarily responsible for the nurture of their children. In these sacred responsibilities, fathers and mothers are obligated to help one another as equal partners. Disability, death, or other circumstances may necessitate individual adaptation. Extended families should lend support when needed.

We warn that individuals who violate covenants of chastity, who abuse spouse or offspring, or who fail to fulfill family responsibilities will one day stand accountable before God. Further, we warn that the disintegration of the family will bring upon individuals, communities, and nations the calamities foretold by ancient and modern prophets.

We call upon responsible citizens and officers of government everywhere to promote those measures designed to maintain and strengthen the family as the fundamental unit of society.

September 23, 1995

CHAPTER 19

OBEYING THE LAWS OF THE LAND

In the early days of the Church, after the saints had been driven, mobbed and plundered over a number of years without protection by government, some of them began to have doubts as to whether or not they should maintain loyalty and allegiance to the government of the United States of America.

In 1842, in what is known as the "Wentworth Letter," the Prophet Joseph Smith wrote what are now known as "The Articles of Faith." In the twelfth article we read, "We believe in being subject to kings, presidents, rulers, and magistrates, in obeying, honoring, and sustaining the law." Also, several years earlier, in what is now known as Doctrine and Covenants 134, members of the Church were reminded that "We believe that governments were instituted of God for the benefit of man." (D&C 134:1) This statement of belief and church doctrine served also as a reply to the accusation at that time that the Latter-day Saints did not support law and order.

Likewise, in our day, as some members of the Church note the decay in moral law fostered by laws and policies of many governments throughout the world, they may begin to wonder whether or not they should support such governments or even be subject to them. The Proclamation is "to the world" and as such includes the saints in all nations. It clearly teaches that we should "be law-abiding citizens wherever [we] live." Again, the Lord has "spoken" on a current issue.

A PROCLAMATION TO THE WORLD

THE FIRST PRESIDENCY AND COUNCIL OF THE TWELVE APOSTLES
OF THE CHURCH OF JESUS CHRIST OF LATTER-DAY SAINTS

We, the First Presidency and the council of the Twelve Apostles of The Church of Jesus Christ of Latter-day Saints, solemnly proclaim that marriage between a man and a woman is ordained of God and that the family is central to the Creator's plan for the eternal destiny of His children.

All human beings—male and female—are created in the image of God. Each is a beloved spirit son or daughter of heavenly parents, and, as such, each has a divine nature and destiny. Gender is an essential characteristic of individual premortal, mortal, and eternal identity and purpose.

In the premortal realm, spirit sons and daughters knew and worshiped God as their eternal Father and accepted His plan by which His children could obtain a physical body and gain earthly experience to progress toward perfection and ultimately realize his or her divine destiny as an heir of eternal life. The divine plan of happiness enables family relationships to be perpetuated beyond the grave. Sacred ordinances and covenants available in holy temples make it possible for individuals to return to the presence of God and for families to be united eternally.

The first commandment that God gave to Adam and Eve pertained to their potential for parenthood as husband and wife. We declare that God's commandment for His children to multiply and replenish the earth remains in force. We further declare that God has commanded that the sacred powers of procreation are to be employed only between man and woman, lawfully wedded as husband and wife.

We declare the means by which mortal life is created to be divinely appointed. We affirm the sanctity of life and of its importance in God's eternal plan.

Husband and wife have a solemn responsibility to love and care for each other and for their children. "Children are an heritage of the Lord." (Psalms 127:3.)

Parents have a sacred duty to rear their children in love and righteousness, to provide for their physical and spiritual needs, to **teach them to love and serve one another, to observe the commandments of God** and to be law-abiding citizens wherever they live. **Husbands and wives—mothers and fathers—will be held accountable before God for the discharge of these obligations.**

The family is ordained of God. Marriage between man and woman is essential to His eternal plan. Children are entitled to birth within the bonds of matrimony, and to be reared by a father and a mother who honor marital vows with complete fidelity. Happiness in family life is most likely to be achieved when founded upon the teachings of the Lord Jesus Christ. Successful marriages and families are established and maintained on principles of faith, prayer, repentance, forgiveness, respect, love, compassion, work, and wholesome recreational activities. By divine design, fathers are to preside over their families in love and righteousness and are responsible to provide the necessities of life and protection of their families. Mothers are primarily responsible for the nurture of their children. In these sacred responsibilities, fathers and mothers are obligated to help one another as equal partners. Disability, death, or other circumstances may necessitate individual adaptation. Extended families should lend support when needed.

We warn that individuals who violate covenants of chastity, who abuse spouse or offspring, or who fail to fulfill family responsibilities will one day stand accountable before God. Further, we warn that the disintegration of the family will bring upon individuals, communities, and nations the calamities foretold by ancient and modern prophets.

We call upon responsible citizens and officers of government everywhere to promote those measures designed to maintain and strengthen the family as the fundamental unit of society.

September 23, 1995

CHAPTER 20

ACCOUNTABILITY FOR PROVIDING RIGHTEOUS HOMES

While it may at first seem like belaboring the point to have these two sentences of the Proclamation singled out as a separate topic for consideration, a closer look reveals that this is a most important issue. The transition from being married with no children to being married with children can be quite a "culture shock." It is wonderful and brings with it much of delight and gratitude; nevertheless, it often requires a change of focus in many forms, not the least of which are the reallocation of financial resources and time.

Thus, in some cases, various forms of rationalization serve to temporarily lessen parents' feelings of accountability to God for the teaching of their children to understand and practice principles of righteousness. This rationalization may come in the form of both parents' working in order to keep up a preferred standard of living. It may take on the disguise of letting the TV or other forms of media take over the high-energy demands of providing meaningful activities and service opportunities for children at home. Or it may come in the form of overemphasizing "self actualization" or personal needs.

Jesus is an example of one who fully accepted the stresses and demands which accompany accountability for the welfare of others. It is not imagination that the Savior was bone-tired as He slept in the ship which was being tossed by the storm to the point that "the ship was covered with the waves." (Matt. 8:24) He was indeed fast asleep, worn out by selfless service to others.

King Benjamin reminds us that the Savior was subject to physical weariness in Mosiah 3:7 when he teaches, "And lo, he shall suffer temptations, and pain of body, hunger, thirst, and fatigue, even more than man can suffer, except it be unto death; for behold, blood cometh from every pore, so great shall be his anguish for the wickedness and the abominations of his people."

Thus, when the Lord asks parents nowadays to accept accountability for providing righteous homes, He does so as one who has worked with His "children" under any and all circumstances, including fatigue, sorrow, happiness, joy, pain, hunger, thirst, temptation, and, in His case, death at the hands of some He loved. He knows as one who has experienced the joy and satisfaction of giving his all to bless others. Isaiah 53:11 speaks of the Savior as it says, "He shall see of the travail of his soul, and shall be satisfied."

Thus, when the Proclamation reminds us of the accountability for providing righteous homes in a world where many do not even make the attempt, it is not placing an undue burden upon parents; rather, it is opening a door to present and future "satisfaction."

A PROCLAMATION TO THE WORLD

THE FIRST PRESIDENCY AND COUNCIL OF THE TWELVE APOSTLES
OF THE CHURCH OF JESUS CHRIST OF LATTER-DAY SAINTS

We, the First Presidency and the council of the Twelve Apostles of The Church of Jesus Christ of Latter-day Saints, solemnly proclaim that marriage between a man and a woman is ordained of God and that the family is central to the Creator's plan for the eternal destiny of His children.

All human beings—male and female—are created in the image of God. Each is a beloved spirit son or daughter of heavenly parents, and, as such, each has a divine nature and destiny. Gender is an essential characteristic of individual premortal, mortal, and eternal identity and purpose.

In the premortal realm, spirit sons and daughters knew and worshiped God as their eternal Father and accepted His plan by which His children could obtain a physical body and gain earthly experience to progress toward perfection and ultimately realize his or her divine destiny as an heir of eternal life. The divine plan of happiness enables family relationships to be perpetuated beyond the grave. Sacred ordinances and covenants available in holy temples make it possible for individuals to return to the presence of God and for families to be united eternally.

The first commandment that God gave to Adam and Eve pertained to their potential for parenthood as husband and wife. We declare that God's commandment for His children to multiply and replenish the earth remains in force. We further declare that God has commanded that the sacred powers of procreation are to be employed only between man and woman, lawfully wedded as husband and wife.

We declare the means by which mortal life is created to be divinely appointed. We affirm the sanctity of life and of its importance in God's eternal plan.

Husband and wife have a solemn responsibility to love and care for each other and for their children. "Children are an heritage of the Lord." (Psalms 127:3.)

Parents have a sacred duty to rear their children in love and righteousness, to **provide for their physical and spiritual needs, to teach them to love and serve one another, to observe the commandments** of God and to be **law-abiding citizens** wherever they live. Husbands and wives—mothers and fathers—will be held accountable before God for the discharge of these obligations.

The family is ordained of God. Marriage between man and woman is essential to His eternal plan. Children are entitled to birth within the bonds of matrimony, and to be reared by a father and a mother who honor marital vows with complete fidelity. **Happiness in family life is most likely to be achieved when founded upon the teachings of the Lord Jesus Christ. Successful marriages and families are established and maintained on principles of faith, prayer, repentance, forgiveness, respect, love, compassion, work, and wholesome recreational activities.** By divine design, fathers are to preside over their families in love and righteousness and are responsible to provide the necessities of life and protection of their families. Mothers are primarily responsible for the nurture of their children. In these sacred responsibilities, fathers and mothers are obligated to help one another as equal partners. Disability, death, or other circumstances may necessitate individual adaptation. Extended families should lend support when needed.

We warn that individuals who violate covenants of chastity, who abuse spouse or offspring, or who fail to fulfill family responsibilities will one day stand accountable before God. Further, we warn that the disintegration of the family will bring upon individuals, communities, and nations the calamities foretold by ancient and modern prophets.

We call upon responsible citizens and officers of government everywhere to promote those measures designed to maintain and strengthen the family as the fundamental unit of society.

September 23, 1995

CHAPTER 21

INGREDIENTS OF RIGHTEOUS HOMES

In the last chapter we spoke of the "accountability" parents have to provide righteous homes. The Lord gave a number of suggestions in the Proclamation to help with this. He explained that such homes are established and maintained upon "principles." This is sometimes referred to as "principle-based management." Joseph Smith explained how he governed such large numbers of people with differing personalities and backgrounds. He said, "I teach them correct principles, and they govern themselves." (*Millennial Star*, 13, Nov. 15, 1851, page 339)

Certainly, children of varying ages and personalities need a "sliding scale" of limits and restraints, consequences and encouragements in order to apply principles. King Benjamin reminds parents of this when he says, "And ye will not suffer your children that they go hungry, or naked; neither will ye suffer that they transgress the laws of God, and fight and quarrel one with another, and serve the devil." (Mosiah 4:14)

The Proclamation focuses on several aspects of righteous homes, including:

1. Providing for their physical needs. Certainly this would include, where possible, adequate clothing, balanced nutrition, physical cleanliness, adequate health care and a clean place to live and sleep. Obviously, conditions in the world vary but with conscientious effort, most of these conditions can be met.

2. Providing for their spiritual needs. This would hopefully include basics such as attending church, personal and family prayer, personal and family scripture reading, payment of an honest tithe, family councils, the opportunity to speak and be heard as respected individuals, plus many other aspects which could be mentioned.

3. Teaching them to love and serve one another. Teaching by example is one of the most powerful ways to teach this.

4. Observe the commandments of God. Again, example is the best teacher.

5. Be law-abiding citizens. Speaking with respect toward police, teachers, government officials etc. goes a long ways toward instilling respect in the minds of children.

6. Daily living based around the teachings of the Savior. One helpful way of doing this is to make sure there are pictures of the Savior and temples in the home, including children's bedrooms. Frequent use of "I'm sorry." and "May I help you?" go a long way toward establishing Christ-centered homes.

7. The principles of "faith, prayer, repentance, forgiveness, respect, love, compassion, work, and wholesome recreational activities" are mainstays of happy and successful homes.

Over the years, studies have been done to try to determine why some children grow up to become reasonably happy adults and why some don't. The attempt has been made to determine which factors in homes are most likely to achieve this goal. After filtering through myriads of possible contributing factors, it was found that there was one basic "common denominator" which seemed to cross the boundaries of culture and economic status. It was "happy childhood memories." Certainly, following the counsel given in the Proclamation about establishing gospel-centered homes will place families well on the way to providing many happy childhood memories. Note that "wholesome recreational activities" is one of the ingredients for happiness in family life. Sometimes, the chance to laugh and play together can help overcome inadequacies and temporary shortcomings in other aspects of parenting while parents themselves grow in child-raising skills.

A PROCLAMATION TO THE WORLD

THE FIRST PRESIDENCY AND COUNCIL OF THE TWELVE APOSTLES
OF THE CHURCH OF JESUS CHRIST OF LATTER-DAY SAINTS

We, the First Presidency and the council of the Twelve Apostles of The Church of Jesus Christ of Latter-day Saints, solemnly proclaim that marriage between a man and a woman is ordained of God and that the family is central to the Creator's plan for the eternal destiny of His children.

All human beings—male and female—are created in the image of God. Each is a beloved spirit son or daughter of heavenly parents, and, as such, each has a divine nature and destiny. Gender is an essential characteristic of individual premortal, mortal, and eternal identity and purpose.

In the premortal realm, spirit sons and daughters knew and worshiped God as their eternal Father and accepted His plan by which His children could obtain a physical body and gain earthly experience to progress toward perfection and ultimately realize his or her divine destiny as an heir of eternal life. The divine plan of happiness enables family relationships to be perpetuated beyond the grave. Sacred ordinances and covenants available in holy temples make it possible for individuals to return to the presence of God and for families to be united eternally.

The first commandment that God gave to Adam and Eve pertained to their potential for parenthood as husband and wife. We declare that God's commandment for His children to multiply and replenish the earth remains in force. We further declare that God has commanded that the sacred powers of procreation are to be employed only between man and woman, lawfully wedded as husband and wife.

We declare the means by which mortal life is created to be divinely appointed. We affirm the sanctity of life and of its importance in God's eternal plan.

Husband and wife have a solemn responsibility to love and care for each other and for their children. "Children are an heritage of the Lord." (Psalms 127:3.)

Parents have a sacred duty to rear their children in love and righteousness, to provide for their physical and spiritual needs, to teach them to love and serve one another, to observe the commandments of God and to be law-abiding citizens wherever they live. Husbands and wives—mothers and fathers—will be held accountable before God for the discharge of these obligations.

The family is ordained of God. Marriage between man and woman is essential to His eternal plan. **Children are entitled** to birth within the bonds of matrimony, and **to be reared by a father and a mother** who honor marital vows with complete fidelity. Happiness in family life is most likely to be achieved when founded upon the teachings of the Lord Jesus Christ. Successful marriages and families are established and maintained on principles of faith, prayer, repentance, forgiveness, respect, love, compassion, work, and wholesome recreational activities. By divine design, fathers are to preside over their families in love and righteousness and are responsible to provide the necessities of life and protection of their families. Mothers are primarily responsible for the nurture of their children. In these sacred responsibilities, fathers and mothers are obligated to help one another as equal partners. Disability, death, or other circumstances may necessitate individual adaptation. Extended families should lend support when needed.

We warn that individuals who violate covenants of chastity, who abuse spouse or offspring, or who fail to fulfill family responsibilities will one day stand accountable before God. Further, we warn that the disintegration of the family will bring upon individuals, communities, and nations the calamities foretold by ancient and modern prophets.

We call upon responsible citizens and officers of government everywhere to promote those measures designed to maintain and strengthen the family as the fundamental unit of society.

September 23, 1995

CHAPTER 22

PLACEMENT OF OUT-OF-WEDLOCK BABIES

This is a sensitive issue. It is usually a highly-charged emotional issue. It deals with the instincts of motherhood in mothers and grandmothers, aunts and great aunts. It pulls and tugs at fathers and grandfathers and extended family members. The baby, who is at the center of all the talk and decision making has no input. A pure, clean, innocent spirit child of God is soon to be born but cannot "lobby" for the setting which will give him or her the best chance to eventually return home to the Father of all.

So it is that the Lord, through the First Presidency and the Council of the Twelve Apostles has, in effect, "lobbied" for the rights of the unborn child. "Children are entitled . . . to be reared by a father and a mother" is a reaffirmation of the counsel of the Brethren regarding the placement of out-of wedlock babies. The first, and preferred choice of course, is that the couple face the issues of their conduct and marry and establish a home where the child will have a father and mother to raise it. In many cases, with the help of the Atonement of Christ, such a home can be established, temple sealing can eventually be achieved, and the birth parents successfully raise their child in a gospel-centered home where "complete fidelity" abides.

However, in circumstances where such a marriage would most likely end in disaster or is out of the question, placing the baby to be adopted into the home of a faithful couple in the Church so that the baby can be raised by both a righteous father and a faithful mother can be one of the highest forms of love that birth parents can manifest. Such a decision can be heart-wrenching for those placing the baby for adoption, but an understanding of correct doctrine can ease the pain. The following is an example of the value of understanding this correct doctrine.

Many years ago, an angry young man approached his girlfriend, who was pregnant with their baby, and threatened to sue her if she gave the baby up to LDS Social Services for adoption. He told her that he did not love her, but that she was to have the baby and keep it until he found someone to marry he did love. Then, they would adopt and raise the baby, and she could go her separate way unencumbered.

He soon found himself in his stake president's office, preparing to answer what he expected would be rather direct and difficult-to-answer questions. As the president prepared to ask the young man to explain his unrighteous position on the matter, the Spirit alerted him that the father did not understand correct doctrine. Instead of asking his intended questions, the stake president instead tenderly asked, "Why are you so concerned about giving the baby up for adoption?" The young man teared up at the unexpected gentleness and quietly explained, "If she gives my baby up for adoption, I'll never see it again."

Quietly, the stake president explained again that, since he refused to marry the mother, the most loving thing to do would be to place the baby for adoption into a righteous home with a father and mother. Then, through deep and thorough repentance and change, he could eventually be forgiven of his sins, marry in the temple, and eventually end up in exaltation. Likewise, the mother could also obtain forgiveness, marry in the temple, and attain exaltation. Thirdly, the baby, raised in a righteous LDS home could someday marry in the house of the Lord and also, through faithfulness, receive exaltation. Thus, he would indeed see his "baby" again, and they would all dwell in the presence of God in celestial glory forever.

A great burden was visibly lifted. He said, "I didn't understand that. I am terribly sorry. I will call my lawyer right now and withdraw the lawsuit." He did.

In the October 1986 General Conference of the Church, Elder Boyd K. Packer taught,

"True doctrine, understood, changes attitudes and behavior. The study of the doctrines of the gospel will improve behavior quicker that a study of behavior will improve behavior."

Such is the power of correct doctrine, understood. Such is the power of the Proclamation.

THE FAMILY
A PROCLAMATION TO THE WORLD
THE FIRST PRESIDENCY AND COUNCIL OF THE TWELVE APOSTLES
OF THE CHURCH OF JESUS CHRIST OF LATTER-DAY SAINTS

We, the First Presidency and the council of the Twelve Apostles of The Church of Jesus Christ of Latter-day Saints, solemnly proclaim that marriage between a man and a woman is ordained of God and that the family is central to the Creator's plan for the eternal destiny of His children.

All human beings—male and female—are created in the image of God. Each is a beloved spirit son or daughter of heavenly parents, and, as such, each has a divine nature and destiny. **Gender is an essential characteristic of individual premortal, mortal, and eternal identity and purpose.**

In the premortal realm, spirit sons and daughters knew and worshiped God as their eternal Father and accepted His plan by which His children could obtain a physical body and gain earthly experience to progress toward perfection and ultimately realize his or her divine destiny as an heir of eternal life. The divine plan of happiness enables family relationships to be perpetuated beyond the grave. Sacred ordinances and covenants available in holy temples make it possible for individuals to return to the presence of God and for families to be united eternally.

The first commandment that God gave to Adam and Eve pertained to their potential for parenthood as husband and wife. We declare that God's commandment for His children to multiply and replenish the earth remains in force. We further declare that God has commanded that the sacred powers of procreation are to be employed only between man and woman, lawfully wedded as husband and wife.

We declare the means by which mortal life is created to be divinely appointed. We affirm the sanctity of life and of its importance in God's eternal plan.

Husband and wife have a solemn responsibility to love and care for each other and for their children. "Children are an heritage of the Lord." (Psalms 127:3.)

Parents have a sacred duty to rear their children in love and righteousness, to provide for their physical and spiritual needs, to teach them to love and serve one another, to observe the commandments of God and to be law-abiding citizens wherever they live. Husbands and wives—mothers and fathers—will be held accountable before God for the discharge of these obligations.

The family is ordained of God. Marriage between man and woman is essential to His eternal plan. Children are entitled to birth within the bonds of matrimony, and to be reared by a father and a mother who honor marital vows with complete fidelity. Happiness in family life is most likely to be achieved when founded upon the teachings of the Lord Jesus Christ. Successful marriages and families are established and maintained on principles of faith, prayer, repentance, forgiveness, respect, love, compassion, work, and wholesome recreational activities. **By divine design, fathers are to preside over their families in love and righteousness and are responsible to provide the necessities of life and protection of their families.** Mothers are primarily responsible for the nurture of their children. In these sacred responsibilities, **fathers and mothers are obligated to help one another** as equal partners. Disability, death, or other circumstances may necessitate individual adaptation. Extended families should lend support when needed.

We warn that individuals who violate covenants of chastity, who abuse spouse or offspring, or **who fail to fulfill family responsibilities will one day stand accountable before God**. Further, we warn that the disintegration of the family will bring upon individuals, communities, and nations the calamities foretold by ancient and modern prophets.

We call upon responsible citizens and officers of government everywhere to promote those measures designed to maintain and strengthen the family as the fundamental unit of society.

September 23, 1995

CHAPTER 23

THE ROLE AND RESPONSIBILITY
OF FATHERS

We speak often of "mother's intuition" and of "maternal instinct." Unfortunately, we don't hear as much about "paternal instinct," the instinct to provide for, train, and protect. Obviously, there is considerable overlap between mother's intuition and father's instinct, and thus the roles of fathers and mothers vary considerably within each family. Yet, in the Proclamation, the Lord makes it clear that each has a divinely (God-given) appointed role.

The word "preside" as used to describe one of the roles of fathers must be handled very carefully. It must not be taken out of the context of the Proclamation where the phrase "fathers and mothers are obligated to help one another as equal partners" also resides. How can one "preside" and still be "equal" with the other? The answer is simple. They are equal. They are equal partners. In "presiding," the husband simply has the added responsibility to see that the mutual decisions of the "equal partnership" succeed. As an inherited gender trait, men tend to be more task-oriented, and it fits their competitive nature to ensure success in goals which are made. An example may help.

In a ward organization, the bishop is called to preside. He participates in councils with other key leaders in the ward. Together, they set goals and make plans to achieve those goals so that all within the ward benefit from the Lord's plan of salvation. As the "presiding officer," the Bishop has the responsibility to see that the plans are carried out, once they have been made by the councils. If he were to try to make all the plans and were to assume the role of "boss," riding rough-shod over the desires and feelings of others, things would quickly fail and fall apart. Soon, it would be "Amen to the priesthood or the authority of that man." (D&C 121:37)

So also in the family unit. A father who is taking on the role of "boss" does not understand the word "preside" nor does he understand D&C 121. And if he does not change, he soon becomes one who exercises "unrighteous dominion" (D&C 121:39). "Preside" implies service. The Savior was the supreme example of one who presides. He served. He gave His all for the blessing and comfort of others. He washed the tired, dusty feet of weary apostles. He forgave and encouraged. He provided food and nourishment. Such is the role of a righteous father.

The father's role as provider often requires that he make personal sacrifices in order to gain adequate education, and training to provide a living for his family. Sometimes, a husband must take or keep employment which does not provide as much money as he would like, yet does provide security and a reliable income over the years around which the family can carefully budget in order to meet basic needs. Some fathers keep "chasing rainbows" in a search for better employment to the extent that it becomes a way of life. They never settle down, thus leaving wife and children in a state of constant anxiousness about finances and security.

The role of "protector" can be viewed in many ways. Physical protection may not be as big an issue in developed nations as it was in times past. Providing adequate housing and clothing is essential. Guarding and protecting the home and family from spiritual danger has become the real battle front in most cases. Additionally, fathers should be approachable to wife and children in terms of emotional needs. A father's laughter and smiles and general pleasantness does much to provide a "protected" environment for his family.

Since individual circumstances vary widely, each father should pray for constant guidance in understanding how he can best fulfill these simple basics for his wife and children, as given in the Proclamation.

A PROCLAMATION TO THE WORLD

THE FIRST PRESIDENCY AND COUNCIL OF THE TWELVE APOSTLES
OF THE CHURCH OF JESUS CHRIST OF LATTER-DAY SAINTS

We, the First Presidency and the council of the Twelve Apostles of The Church of Jesus Christ of Latter-day Saints, solemnly proclaim that marriage between a man and a woman is ordained of God and that the family is central to the Creator's plan for the eternal destiny of His children.

All human beings—male and female—are created in the image of God. Each is a beloved spirit son or daughter of heavenly parents, and, as such, each has a divine nature and destiny. **Gender is an essential characteristic of individual premortal, mortal, and eternal identity and purpose.**

In the premortal realm, spirit sons and daughters knew and worshiped God as their eternal Father and accepted His plan by which His children could obtain a physical body and gain earthly experience to progress toward perfection and ultimately realize his or her divine destiny as an heir of eternal life. The divine plan of happiness enables family relationships to be perpetuated beyond the grave. Sacred ordinances and covenants available in holy temples make it possible for individuals to return to the presence of God and for families to be united eternally.

The first commandment that God gave to Adam and Eve pertained to their potential for parenthood as husband and wife. We declare that God's commandment for His children to multiply and replenish the earth remains in force. We further declare that God has commanded that the sacred powers of procreation are to be employed only between man and woman, lawfully wedded as husband and wife.

We declare the means by which mortal life is created to be divinely appointed. We affirm the sanctity of life and of its importance in God's eternal plan.

Husband and wife have a solemn responsibility to love and care for each other and for their children. "Children are an heritage of the Lord." (Psalms 127:3.)

Parents have a sacred duty to rear their children in love and righteousness, to provide for their physical and spiritual needs, to teach them to love and serve one another, to observe the commandments of God and to be law-abiding citizens wherever they live. Husbands and wives—mothers and fathers—will be held accountable before God for the discharge of these obligations.

The family is ordained of God. Marriage between man and woman is essential to His eternal plan. Children are entitled to birth within the bonds of matrimony, and to be reared by a father and a mother who honor marital vows with complete fidelity. Happiness in family life is most likely to be achieved when founded upon the teachings of the Lord Jesus Christ. Successful marriages and families are established and maintained on principles of faith, prayer, repentance, forgiveness, respect, love, compassion, work, and wholesome recreational activities. **By divine design,** fathers are to preside over their families in love and righteousness and are responsible to provide the necessities of life and protection of their families. **Mothers are primarily responsible for the nurture of their children.** In these sacred responsibilities, **fathers and mothers are obligated to help one another as equal partners.** Disability, death, or other circumstances may necessitate individual adaptation. Extended families should lend support when needed.

We warn that individuals who violate covenants of chastity, who abuse spouse or offspring, or **who fail to fulfill family responsibilities will one day stand accountable before God.** Further, we warn that the disintegration of the family will bring upon individuals, communities, and nations the calamities foretold by ancient and modern prophets.

We call upon responsible citizens and officers of government everywhere to promote those measures designed to maintain and strengthen the family as the fundamental unit of society.

September 23, 1995

CHAPTER 24

THE ROLE AND RESPONSIBILITIES
OF MOTHERS

Perhaps you have noticed that the Proclamation is a "principle-based" document. By "principle-based" we mean a document which does not have a lot of detailed explanation. Rather, it presents basic principles which serve as guidelines in any number of settings and circumstances. The fewer the details given, the broader the territory covered by the principle. For example, "Be honest" is a principle-based statement. It applies to a person in private, in public, in business dealings, in politics, with the Lord and with everyone else, in all places, and at all times. "Keep the Sabbath Day holy" is a principle-based commandment to honor the Sabbath. Many members of the Church wish for more detail about keeping the Sabbath Day holy. Too much detail would limit it and ultimately ruin it, much as was the case with the Jews at the time of the Savior's ministry among them. The Word of Wisdom is "a principle with a promise." (D&C 89:3) So also is "Mothers are primarily responsible for the nurture of their children" a "principle with a promise," the promise of the highest satisfaction and happiness here and in eternity.

There are but two key elements in this statement, "primarily responsible" and "nurture." Yet, they are all-encompassing, another testimony of the inspired nature of the Proclamation. "Primarily responsible" is a statement of fact, a state of being, a confirmation of woman's natural capacity to nourish, a reminder that one of the gender gifts to women is a natural skill to meet needs of children.

"Nurture" is an action verb. How many ways are there for a mother to "nurture" her children? How many needs can children have growing up? How much nurture is needed physically, emotionally, spiritually, intellectually? How many days need brightening? How many bright days need sharing? How many hugs? How many long chats? How many goodbyes? How many hellos? How many bandages? How many kiss-it-betters? The list is infinite.

In how many settings, cultures, and economic circumstances can she accomplish her divine role? The answer? "All." There is much truth in the old saying, "The hand that rocks the cradle rules the nation."

Among many other things, the Proclamation is a reminder that both mothers and fathers should do all in their power to prioritize such that the divine nature of womanhood and motherhood can be comprehensive in the raising of their children.

A PROCLAMATION TO THE WORLD

THE FIRST PRESIDENCY AND COUNCIL OF THE TWELVE APOSTLES
OF THE CHURCH OF JESUS CHRIST OF LATTER-DAY SAINTS

We, the First Presidency and the council of the Twelve Apostles of The Church of Jesus Christ of Latter-day Saints, solemnly proclaim that marriage between a man and a woman is ordained of God and that the family is central to the Creator's plan for the eternal destiny of His children.

All human beings—male and female—are created in the image of God. Each is a beloved spirit son or daughter of heavenly parents, and, as such, each has a divine nature and destiny. Gender is an essential characteristic of individual premortal, mortal, and eternal identity and purpose.

In the premortal realm, spirit sons and daughters knew and worshiped God as their eternal Father and accepted His plan by which His children could obtain a physical body and gain earthly experience to progress toward perfection and ultimately realize his or her divine destiny as an heir of eternal life. The divine plan of happiness enables family relationships to be perpetuated beyond the grave. Sacred ordinances and covenants available in holy temples make it possible for individuals to return to the presence of God and for families to be united eternally.

The first commandment that God gave to Adam and Eve pertained to their potential for parenthood as husband and wife. We declare that God's commandment for His children to multiply and replenish the earth remains in force. We further declare that God has commanded that the sacred powers of procreation are to be employed only between man and woman, lawfully wedded as husband and wife.

We declare the means by which mortal life is created to be divinely appointed. We affirm the sanctity of life and of its importance in God's eternal plan.

Husband and wife have a solemn responsibility to love and care for each other and for their children. "Children are an heritage of the Lord." (Psalms 127:3.)

Parents have a sacred duty to rear their children in love and righteousness, to provide for their physical and spiritual needs, to teach them to **love and serve one another, to observe the commandments of God and to be law-abiding citizens wherever they live.** Husbands and wives—mothers and fathers—will be held accountable before God for the discharge of these obligations.

The family is ordained of God. Marriage between man and woman is essential to His eternal plan. Children are entitled to birth within the bonds of matrimony, and to be reared by a father and a mother who honor marital vows with complete fidelity. **Happiness in family life is most likely to be achieved when founded upon the teachings of the Lord Jesus Christ. Successful marriages and families are established and maintained on principles of faith, prayer, repentance, forgiveness, respect, love, compassion, work, and wholesome   recreational activities.** By divine design, fathers are to preside over their families in love and righteousness and are responsible to provide the necessities of life and protection of their families. Mothers are primarily responsible for the nurture of their children. In these sacred responsibilities, fathers and mothers are obligated to help one another as equal partners. Disability, death, or other circumstances may necessitate individual adaptation. Extended families should lend support when needed.

We warn that individuals who violate covenants of chastity, who abuse spouse or offspring, or who fail to fulfill family responsibilities will one day stand accountable before God. Further, we warn that the disintegration of the family will bring upon individuals, communities, and nations the calamities foretold by ancient and modern prophets.

We call upon responsible citizens and officers of government everywhere to promote those measures designed to maintain and strengthen the family as the fundamental unit of society.

September 23, 1995

CHAPTER 25

THE ROLE OF CHILDREN

Certainly the role of children as implied in the Proclamation ought not to be left out. Children have an obvious obligation to do their part and to sustain their parents in establishing "happiness in family life" in their homes.

Guidelines for children, as pointed out in the copy of the Proclamation marked for this chapter, include:

1. Loving and serving one another.
2. Observing the commandments of God.
3. Being law-abiding citizens in whatever country they live.
4. Learning and understanding the teachings of the Lord Jesus Christ.
5. Establishing and maintaining, in their own attitudes and behaviors, the principles of faith, prayer, repentance, forgiveness, respect, love, compassion, work, and participating with their families in wholesome recreational activities.

For whatever reasons, it seems to have become an expectation on the part of many children that it is the parent's responsibility to entertain them and satisfy their every need. The Proclamation serves as an important reminder that this is not necessarily the case. Perhaps many parents inadvertently foster this attitude on the part of their children by not giving them enough responsibility around home and expecting accountability. D&C 68:25 instructs us that children are capable of understanding "the doctrine of repentance, faith in Christ the Son of the living God, and of baptism and the gift of the Holy Ghost by the laying on of the hands" by the time they are eight years old. It is at that point that they "begin to become accountable before me." (D&C 29:47) If they are to have learned these vital teachings by the time they are eight, and since they begin to become accountable for their own behaviors at that point, it is obvious that they have a responsibility to assist parents in establishing a pleasant, righteous home. This responsibility continues on through teenage years and beyond.

A PROCLAMATION TO THE WORLD

THE FIRST PRESIDENCY AND COUNCIL OF THE TWELVE APOSTLES
OF THE CHURCH OF JESUS CHRIST OF LATTER-DAY SAINTS

We, the First Presidency and the council of the Twelve Apostles of The Church of Jesus Christ of Latter-day Saints, solemnly proclaim that marriage between a man and a woman is ordained of God and that the family is central to the Creator's plan for the eternal destiny of His children.

All human beings—male and female—are created in the image of God. Each is a beloved spirit son or daughter of heavenly parents, and, as such, each has a divine nature and destiny. Gender is an essential characteristic of individual premortal, mortal, and eternal identity and purpose.

In the premortal realm, spirit sons and daughters knew and worshiped God as their eternal Father and accepted His plan by which His children could obtain a physical body and gain earthly experience to progress toward perfection and ultimately realize his or her divine destiny as an heir of eternal life. The divine plan of happiness enables family relationships to be perpetuated beyond the grave. Sacred ordinances and covenants available in holy temples make it possible for individuals to return to the presence of God and for families to be united eternally.

The first commandment that God gave to Adam and Eve pertained to their potential for parenthood as husband and wife. We declare that God's commandment for His children to multiply and replenish the earth remains in force. We further declare that God has commanded that the sacred powers of procreation are to be employed only between man and woman, lawfully wedded as husband and wife.

We declare the means by which mortal life is created to be divinely appointed. We affirm the sanctity of life and of its importance in God's eternal plan.

Husband and wife have a solemn responsibility to love and care for each other and for their children. "Children are an heritage of the Lord." (Psalms 127:3.)

Parents have a sacred duty to rear their children in love and righteousness, to provide for their physical and spiritual needs, to teach them to love and serve one another, to observe the commandments of God and to be law-abiding citizens wherever they live. Husbands and wives—mothers and fathers—will be held accountable before God for the discharge of these obligations.

The family is ordained of God. Marriage between man and woman is essential to His eternal plan. Children are entitled to birth within the bonds of matrimony, and to be reared by a father and a mother who honor marital vows with complete fidelity. Happiness in family life is most likely to be achieved when founded upon the teachings of the Lord Jesus Christ. Successful marriages and families are established and maintained on principles of faith, prayer, repentance, forgiveness, respect, love, compassion, work, and wholesome recreational activities. By divine design, fathers are to preside over their families in love and righteousness and are responsible to provide the necessities of life and protection of their families. Mothers are primarily responsible for the nurture of their children. In these sacred responsibilities, **fathers and mothers are** obligated to help one another **as equal partners.** Disability, death, or other circumstances may necessitate individual adaptation. Extended families should lend support when needed.

We warn that individuals who violate covenants of chastity, who abuse spouse or offspring, or who fail to fulfill family responsibilities will one day stand accountable before God. Further, we warn that the disintegration of the family will bring upon individuals, communities, and nations the calamities foretold by ancient and modern prophets.

We call upon responsible citizens and officers of government everywhere to promote those measures designed to maintain and strengthen the family as the fundamental unit of society.

September 23, 1995

CHAPTER 26

THE EQUALITY OF FATHERS AND MOTHERS

Perhaps few issues have been as divisive and heated over the past several years as the issue of equality between men and women, husbands and wives. Volumes have been written. Countless debates and arguments have arisen. Anger, emotion, reason, ridicule, bitter accusation, passionate rebuttal, all have been used to attempt to further the cause of one side or the other. Through it all comes the calm voice of the Lord, speaking quietly through our prophets and apostles, with a clear, sweet fact—an eternal doctrine: "Fathers and mothers . . . are equal partners."

This statement in the Proclamation is profound! Once we understand and accept this truth, this eternal doctrine, all that remains for us to do is to act accordingly in our behavior toward each other. With true doctrine in our minds and hearts, the debate is over. All our energies, which might have gone into debate and argument on the issue of equality, can now be used to sustain each other as "equal partners."

D&C 132 also teaches the equality of husbands and wives who, together, attain exaltation and thus become gods. After reading D&C 132:19, read verse 20, paying close attention to **the pronouns which refer to both the husband and the wife.** We will include verse 20 here and put the pronouns in bold so they stand out a bit more.

> Then shall **they** be gods, because **they** have no end; therefore shall **they** be from everlasting to everlasting, because **they** continue; then shall **they** be above all, because all things are subject unto **them.** Then shall **they** be gods, because **they** have all power, and the angels are subject unto **them.**

In *Mormon Doctrine*, page 613, Elder Bruce R. McConkie explained the above verse as follows: "If righteous men have power through the gospel and its crowning ordinance of celestial marriage to become kings and priests to rule in exaltation forever, it follows that the women by their side (without whom they cannot attain exaltation) will be queens and priestesses. (Rev. 1:6; 5:10) Exaltation grows out of the eternal union of a man and his wife. Of those whose marriage endures in eternity, the Lord says, "Then shall they be gods" (D&C 132:20); that is, each of them, the man and the woman, will be a god. As such they will rule over their dominions forever (*Mormon Doctrine*, 2d ed. Salt Lake City: Bookcraft, 1966, 613).

Once again the understanding of true doctrine can change behavior very quickly, as taught by Elder Boyd K. Packer in the October 1986 General Conference when he explained, "True doctrine, understood, changes attitudes and behavior. The study of the doctrines of the gospel will improve behavior quicker than a study of behavior will improve behavior."

Perhaps a bit more on this important topic would be helpful. Ephesians 5:22-24 is often quoted out of context with resulting damage and hurt to both women and men on the issue of equality. These verses are as follows:

> 22 Wives, submit yourselves unto your own husbands, as unto the Lord.

> 23 For the husband is the head of the wife, even as Christ is the head of the church: and he is the saviour of the body.

> 24 Therefore as the church is subject unto Christ, so let the wives be to their own husbands in every thing.

Various translations and explanations of Paul's words in verses 22-24 often cause confusion and resentment. When we come to such verses in the Bible, where misinterpretation and misunderstanding are possible, we need to step back and ask ourselves, "What do our current prophets teach us respecting this topic?" There is safety in following the Brethren. What do the Brethren say on the topic of equality of husbands and wives? The answer is clear. In addition to what the Proclamation says, President James E. Faust said in the April 1988 General Conference, "Nowhere does the doctrine of this Church declare that men are superior to women."

President Faust also said,

> "Every father is to his family a patriarch and every mother a matriarch as coequals in their distinctive parental roles." ("The Prophetic Voice," April 1996 General Conference)

President Joseph F. Smith said, referring to parents, "They stand as the head of the family, the patriarch, the mother, the rulers." (*Gospel Doctrine*, published by Deseret Book, 1977, p. 161)

With these quotes before us, it becomes obvious that there is a difference between how priesthood holders "preside" in the Church and the role of priesthood in the home. It is when the role of priesthood in the Church is imposed upon the family, or vice versa, that trouble arises.

Elder Boyd K. Packer explained this difference. He said, "There is a difference in the way the priesthood functions in the home as compared to the way it functions in the Church. . . . In the Church there is a distinct line of authority. . . . In the home it is a partnership with husband and wife equally yoked together, sharing in decisions, always working together." ("The Relief Society," April 1998 General Conference)

Spencer W. Kimball taught about the role of the priesthood holder in the family as follows: "Can you find in all the holy scriptures where the Lord Jesus Christ ever failed his church? Can you find any scripture that says he was untrue to his people, to his neighbors, friends, or associates? Was he faithful? Was he true? Is there anything good and worthy that he did not give? Then that is what we ask—what he asks of a husband, every husband. That is the goal. Can you think of a single exception in his great life? There should be none in yours." (Spencer W. Kimball, Address to Religious Educators in the Assembly Hall, 12 Sept. 1975, pp. 3-5)

The Proclamation reaffirms for some and explains to many others the simple doctrine that husbands and wives, men and women, are equal.

A PROCLAMATION TO THE WORLD

THE FIRST PRESIDENCY AND COUNCIL OF THE TWELVE APOSTLES
OF THE CHURCH OF JESUS CHRIST OF LATTER-DAY SAINTS

We, the First Presidency and the council of the Twelve Apostles of The Church of Jesus Christ of Latter-day Saints, solemnly proclaim that marriage between a man and a woman is ordained of God and that the family is central to the Creator's plan for the eternal destiny of His children.

All human beings—male and female—are created in the image of God. Each is a beloved spirit son or daughter of heavenly parents, and, as such, each has a divine nature and destiny. Gender is an essential characteristic of individual premortal, mortal, and eternal identity and purpose.

In the premortal realm, spirit sons and daughters knew and worshiped God as their eternal Father and accepted His plan by which His children could obtain a physical body and gain earthly experience to progress toward perfection and ultimately realize his or her divine destiny as an heir of eternal life. The divine plan of happiness enables family relationships to be perpetuated beyond the grave. Sacred ordinances and covenants available in holy temples make it possible for individuals to return to the presence of God and for families to be united eternally.

The first commandment that God gave to Adam and Eve pertained to their potential for parenthood as husband and wife. We declare that God's commandment for His children to multiply and replenish the earth remains in force. We further declare that God has commanded that the sacred powers of procreation are to be employed only between man and woman, lawfully wedded as husband and wife.

We declare the means by which mortal life is created to be divinely appointed. We affirm the sanctity of life and of its importance in God's eternal plan.

Husband and wife have a solemn responsibility to love and care for each other and for their children. "Children are an heritage of the Lord." (Psalms 127:3.)

Parents have a sacred duty to rear their children in love and righteousness, to provide for their physical and spiritual needs, to teach them to love and serve one another, to observe the commandments of God and to be law-abiding citizens wherever they live. Husbands and wives—mothers and fathers—will be held accountable before God for the discharge of these obligations.

The family is ordained of God. Marriage between man and woman is essential to His eternal plan. Children are entitled to birth within the bonds of matrimony, and to be reared by a father and a mother who honor marital vows with complete fidelity. Happiness in family life is most likely to be achieved when founded upon the teachings of the Lord Jesus Christ. Successful marriages and families are established and maintained on principles of faith, prayer, repentance, forgiveness, respect, love, compassion, work, and wholesome recreational activities. By divine design, fathers are to preside over their families in love and righteousness and are responsible to provide the necessities of life and protection of their families. Mothers are primarily responsible for the nurture of their children. In these sacred responsibilities, fathers and mothers are obligated to help one another as equal partners. **Disability, death, or other circumstances may necessitate individual adaptation. Extended families should lend support when needed.**

We warn that individuals who violate covenants of chastity, who abuse spouse or offspring, or who fail to fulfill family responsibilities will one day stand accountable before God. Further, we warn that the disintegration of the family will bring upon individuals, communities, and nations the calamities foretold by ancient and modern prophets.

We call upon responsible citizens and officers of government everywhere to promote those measures designed to maintain and strengthen the family as the fundamental unit of society.

September 23, 1995

CHAPTER 27

ADAPTATION FOR OTHER CIRCUMSTANCES

There are many family circumstances which require adaptation and help from others. In some cases, for instance, both parents have been killed in a traffic accident and grandparents are raising the grandchildren. In one case with which I am acquainted, both parents died from separate illnesses and the older siblings raised the younger ones. Divorce, separation, the death of one spouse, illness, disability or any one of several other possibilities can temporarily change the form of the family unit.

As we read this statement in the Proclamation, we are assured of the value of families whose circumstances require adaptation. They are included in the "word of the Lord" here. Among other things, we come to understand that the Lord expects His saints to help each other out. There have been many articles in recent Ensign Magazines which have described such special situations and have told of the blessings which come as others assist.

The ward or branch "family" often becomes one of the most helpful "extended families" to help supplement and fill in for the missing father or mother. Often, the most critical needs seem to be with single parents with young children or teenagers. Yet, single adults who have never been married, widows or widowers, elderly couples with limited mobility, grandparents and great grandparents can be counted among those whose circumstances require "adaptation."

Correct doctrine about the potential for eternal families can be of great comfort during mortality for single parents and those who have never married or have married but have been unable to have children. Through their faithfulness, they are assured that all of the blessings of a family unit in eternity will someday be theirs.

Brigham Young provided comforting words to all in the Church whose dreams of family and children have not yet come to be.

"Let me here say a word to console the feelings and hearts of all who belong to this Church. Many of the sisters grieve because they are not blessed with offspring. You will see the time when you will have millions of children around you. If you are faithful to your covenants, you will be mothers of nations. You will become Eves to earths like this, and when you have assisted in peopling one earth, there are millions of others still in the course of creation. And when they have endured a thousand million times longer than this earth, it is only as it were at the beginning of your creation. Be faithful and if you are not blessed with children in this time, you will be hereafter." (Deseret News, Vol. 10, p. 306, October 14, 1860)

Spencer W. Kimball was concerned that the constant emphasis given in church meetings on traditional family and children can be painful to those faithful members who have not yet achieved this goal. He said:

"We have no choice . . . but to continue to hold up the ideal of the Latter-day Saint family. The fact that some do not now have the privilege of living in such a family is not reason enough to stop talking about it. We do discuss family life with sensitivity, however, realizing that many . . . do not presently have the privilege of belonging or contributing to such a family. But we cannot set aside this standard, because so many other things depend upon it" (Kimball, Teachings of Spencer W. Kimball, pp. 294–95).

He went on to say to faithful single sisters,

"In the meantime, we promise you that insofar as your eternity is concerned, that no soul will be deprived of rich, eternal blessings for anything which that person could not help, that eternity is a long time, and that the Lord never fails in his promises and that every righteous woman will receive eventually all to which she is entitled which she has not forfeited through any fault of her own" (Kimball, Teachings of Spencer W. Kimball, p. 294)

It is often pointed out that this mortal life is but a brief moment in eternity. Certainly, that is true. Nevertheless, for those whose find themselves struggling with extra stresses and the responsibilities which are normally shared by two parents, or for those singles who pray daily for the blessing of marriage and family, this mortal "moment in eternity" seems like "an eternal moment." Faith to continue loyal to God at all costs is bolstered by testimony and the sure knowledge that all the blessings of exaltation will ultimately come to the faithful.

THE FAMILY
A PROCLAMATION TO THE WORLD
THE FIRST PRESIDENCY AND COUNCIL OF THE TWELVE APOSTLES
OF THE CHURCH OF JESUS CHRIST OF LATTER-DAY SAINTS

We, the First Presidency and the council of the Twelve Apostles of The Church of Jesus Christ of Latter-day Saints, solemnly proclaim that marriage between a man and a woman is ordained of God and that the family is central to the Creator's plan for the eternal destiny of His children.

All human beings—male and female—are created in the image of God. Each is a beloved spirit son or daughter of heavenly parents, and, as such, each has a divine nature and destiny. Gender is an essential characteristic of individual premortal, mortal, and eternal identity and purpose.

In the premortal realm, spirit sons and daughters knew and worshiped God as their eternal Father and accepted His plan by which His children could obtain a physical body and gain earthly experience to progress toward perfection and ultimately realize his or her divine destiny as an heir of eternal life. The divine plan of happiness enables family relationships to be perpetuated beyond the grave. Sacred ordinances and covenants available in holy temples make it possible for individuals to return to the presence of God and for families to be united eternally.

The first commandment that God gave to Adam and Eve pertained to their potential for parenthood as husband and wife. We declare that God's commandment for His children to multiply and replenish the earth remains in force. We further declare that God has commanded that the sacred powers of procreation are to be employed only between man and woman, lawfully wedded as husband and wife.

We declare the means by which mortal life is created to be divinely appointed. We affirm the sanctity of life and of its importance in God's eternal plan.

Husband and wife have a solemn responsibility to love and care for each other and for their children. "Children are an heritage of the Lord." (Psalms 127:3.)

Parents have a sacred duty to rear their children in love and righteousness, to provide for their physical and spiritual needs, to teach them to love and serve one another, to observe the commandments of God and to be law-abiding citizens wherever they live. Husbands and wives—mothers and fathers—will be held accountable before God for the discharge of these obligations.

The family is ordained of God. Marriage between man and woman is essential to His eternal plan. Children are entitled to birth within the bonds of matrimony, and to be reared by a father and a mother who honor marital vows with complete fidelity. Happiness in family life is most likely to be achieved when founded upon the teachings of the Lord Jesus Christ. Successful marriages and families are established and maintained on principles of faith, prayer, repentance, forgiveness, respect, love, compassion, work, and wholesome recreational activities. By divine design, fathers are to preside over their families in love and righteousness and are responsible to provide the necessities of life and protection of their families. Mothers are primarily responsible for the nurture of their children. In these sacred responsibilities, fathers and mothers are obligated to help one another as equal partners. Disability, death, or other circumstances may necessitate individual adaptation. Extended families should lend support when needed.

We warn that individuals who violate covenants of chastity, who abuse spouse or offspring, or who fail to fulfill family responsibilities **will one day stand accountable before God.** Further, we warn that the disintegration of the family will bring upon individuals, communities, and nations the calamities foretold by ancient and modern prophets.

We call upon responsible citizens and officers of government everywhere to promote those measures designed to maintain and strengthen the family as the fundamental unit of society.

September 23, 1995

CHAPTER 28

VIOLATION OF THE LAW OF CHASTITY

The use of the powers of procreation between a man and a woman who love each other and who are married to each other is one of the most powerful and beautiful expressions of commitment and tenderness. Such a relationship strengthens the bond and commitment between husband and wife. As quoted in Chapter 15, Elder Boyd K. Packer refers to such use of the powers of procreation as "the very key" to happiness. This is a very powerful statement. What a blessing it is to have prophets, seers, and revelators who speak plainly on such weighty matters.

At the opposite end of the spectrum we find those who advocate and practice no restraint at all in the use of this sacred power. They are either tragically blind or blatantly greedy and wicked. They either fail to see or deliberately refuse to acknowledge that such abuse of these powers carries with it the sure destruction of civilization as designed by God. History teaches this lesson over and over.

Adultery, fornication, sexual abuse, homosexuality, masturbation, pornography, unchecked lustful thinking, and a whole host of related evils severely damage individuals and those associated with them. There is no such thing as a "victimless" sin. At the very least, any individual who deliberately engages in any form of breaking the law of chastity diminishes his or her capability to be sensitive to the Spirit, thus making those whom they might have otherwise helped and strengthened unwitting victims. No wonder the Lord holds them accountable! Deep, abiding repentance is the only escape. The Proclamation uses strong words to denounce these sins. We will speak more of this in Chapter 31.

One final question. Can one ever become completely clean after having broken the law of chastity? Isaiah 1:18 provides the answer: "Come now, and let us reason together, saith the LORD: though your sins be as scarlet, they shall be as white as snow; though they be red like crimson, they shall be as wool."

It is interesting to note that "scarlet" and "crimson" in the above verse were colorfast dyes in Isaiah's day. Knowing this gives added weight to his words, describing the power of the Atonement of Christ to cleanse and heal even "colorfast sins."

At a BYU Devotional on March 26, 1985, Elder Theodore M. Burton reminded students that the Atonement has the power to restore Chastity. He said,

> "Jesus Christ can restore that virtue and he can thus show you mercy . . . Jesus has power to restore virtue and make your victim absolutely clean and holy."

THE FAMILY

A PROCLAMATION TO THE WORLD

THE FIRST PRESIDENCY AND COUNCIL OF THE TWELVE APOSTLES
OF THE CHURCH OF JESUS CHRIST OF LATTER-DAY SAINTS

We, the First Presidency and the council of the Twelve Apostles of The Church of Jesus Christ of Latter-day Saints, solemnly proclaim that marriage between a man and a woman is ordained of God and that the family is central to the Creator's plan for the eternal destiny of His children.

All human beings—male and female—are created in the image of God. Each is a beloved spirit son or daughter of heavenly parents, and, as such, each has a divine nature and destiny. Gender is an essential characteristic of individual premortal, mortal, and eternal identity and purpose.

In the premortal realm, spirit sons and daughters knew and worshiped God as their eternal Father and accepted His plan by which His children could obtain a physical body and gain earthly experience to progress toward perfection and ultimately realize his or her divine destiny as an heir of eternal life. The divine plan of happiness enables family relationships to be perpetuated beyond the grave. Sacred ordinances and covenants available in holy temples make it possible for individuals to return to the presence of God and for families to be united eternally.

The first commandment that God gave to Adam and Eve pertained to their potential for parenthood as husband and wife. We declare that God's commandment for His children to multiply and replenish the earth remains in force. We further declare that God has commanded that the sacred powers of procreation are to be employed only between man and woman, lawfully wedded as husband and wife.

We declare the means by which mortal life is created to be divinely appointed. We affirm the sanctity of life and of its importance in God's eternal plan.

Husband and wife have a solemn responsibility to love and care for each other and for their children. "Children are an heritage of the Lord." (Psalms 127:3.)

Parents have a sacred duty to rear their children in love and righteousness, to provide for their physical and spiritual needs, to teach them to love and serve one another, to observe the commandments of God and to be law-abiding citizens wherever they live. Husbands and wives—mothers and fathers—will be held accountable before God for the discharge of these obligations.

The family is ordained of God. Marriage between man and woman is essential to His eternal plan. Children are entitled to birth within the bonds of matrimony, and to be reared by a father and a mother who honor marital vows with complete fidelity. Happiness in family life is most likely to be achieved when founded upon the teachings of the Lord Jesus Christ. Successful marriages and families are established and maintained on principles of faith, prayer, repentance, forgiveness, respect, love, compassion, work, and wholesome recreational activities. By divine design, fathers are to preside over their families in love and righteousness and are responsible to provide the necessities of life and protection of their families. Mothers are primarily responsible for the nurture of their children. In these sacred responsibilities, fathers and mothers are obligated to help one another as equal partners. Disability, death, or other circumstances may necessitate individual adaptation. Extended families should lend support when needed.

We warn that individuals who violate covenants of chastity, **who abuse spouse** or offspring, or who fail to fulfill family responsibilities **will one day stand accountable before God.** Further, we warn that the disintegration of the family will bring upon individuals, communities, and nations the calamities foretold by ancient and modern prophets.

We call upon responsible citizens and officers of government everywhere to promote those measures designed to maintain and strengthen the family as the fundamental unit of society.

September 23, 1995

CHAPTER 29

SPOUSE ABUSE

It seems that there is an unwritten law which might be termed "The Law of Mirror Images." Simply put, it is a "law" which says "for everything that promotes the highest good for God's children, Satan sponsors an evil which takes them as far down as obedience to God's commandments lifts them." Another way to put it might be, "for every good sponsored by God, an equal and opposite evil is sponsored by Satan."

For example, the highest good to which God's children are invited is exaltation, or eternal life in the family unit in the presence of the Father. The opposite, sponsored by Lucifer and described in D&C 76:31-35 and elsewhere, is that of becoming a son of perdition.

The Proclamation mentions and emphasizes in many different ways that the family is "the fundamental unit of society." Within a righteous family, the highest Christlike virtues can be developed and nurtured by parents, children, and by the Holy Ghost. Indeed, the qualities of eventual godhood are fostered and learned in a safe environment which provides "a defense" and "a refuge from the storm." (D&C 115:6)

The "mirror image" of this is Satan's way, and would include the horrors of spouse abuse. A home in which such abuse exists is the opposite of the righteous home described in the Proclamation. The ingredients of a happy home are replaced by fear, horror, bitter loneliness, self doubt, hopelessness, a sense of being trapped, and sometimes even the feeling of being less valuable in the eyes of God.

The Brethren speak very strongly as they condemn this evil. Those who practice this pernicious evil will someday stand before the judgment bar of God with "a perfect knowledge of all [their] guilt and [their] uncleanness." (2 Nephi 9:14) This is one of the few sins for which a Church disciplinary council is mandatory.

A PROCLAMATION TO THE WORLD

THE FIRST PRESIDENCY AND COUNCIL OF THE TWELVE APOSTLES
OF THE CHURCH OF JESUS CHRIST OF LATTER-DAY SAINTS

We, the First Presidency and the council of the Twelve Apostles of The Church of Jesus Christ of Latter-day Saints, solemnly proclaim that marriage between a man and a woman is ordained of God and that the family is central to the Creator's plan for the eternal destiny of His children.

All human beings—male and female—are created in the image of God. Each is a beloved spirit son or daughter of heavenly parents, and, as such, each has a divine nature and destiny. Gender is an essential characteristic of individual premortal, mortal, and eternal identity and purpose.

In the premortal realm, spirit sons and daughters knew and worshiped God as their eternal Father and accepted His plan by which His children could obtain a physical body and gain earthly experience to progress toward perfection and ultimately realize his or her divine destiny as an heir of eternal life. The divine plan of happiness enables family relationships to be perpetuated beyond the grave. Sacred ordinances and covenants available in holy temples make it possible for individuals to return to the presence of God and for families to be united eternally.

The first commandment that God gave to Adam and Eve pertained to their potential for parenthood as husband and wife. We declare that God's commandment for His children to multiply and replenish the earth remains in force. We further declare that God has commanded that the sacred powers of procreation are to be employed only between man and woman, lawfully wedded as husband and wife.

We declare the means by which mortal life is created to be divinely appointed. We affirm the sanctity of life and of its importance in God's eternal plan.

Husband and wife have a solemn responsibility to love and care for each other and for their children. "Children are an heritage of the Lord." (Psalms 127:3.)

Parents have a sacred duty to rear their children in love and righteousness, to provide for their physical and spiritual needs, to teach them to love and serve one another, to observe the commandments of God and to be law-abiding citizens wherever they live. Husbands and wives—mothers and fathers—will be held accountable before God for the discharge of these obligations.

The family is ordained of God. Marriage between man and woman is essential to His eternal plan. Children are entitled to birth within the bonds of matrimony, and to be reared by a father and a mother who honor marital vows with complete fidelity. Happiness in family life is most likely to be achieved when founded upon the teachings of the Lord Jesus Christ. Successful marriages and families are established and maintained on principles of faith, prayer, repentance, forgiveness, respect, love, compassion, work, and wholesome recreational activities. By divine design, fathers are to preside over their families in love and righteousness and are responsible to provide the necessities of life and protection of their families. Mothers are primarily responsible for the nurture of their children. In these sacred responsibilities, fathers and mothers are obligated to help one another as equal partners. Disability, death, or other circumstances may necessitate individual adaptation. Extended families should lend support when needed.

We warn that individuals who violate covenants of chastity, **who abuse** spouse or **offspring**, or who fail to fulfill family responsibilities **will one day stand accountable before God.** Further, we warn that the disintegration of the family will bring upon individuals, communities, and nations the calamities foretold by ancient and modern prophets.

We call upon responsible citizens and officers of government everywhere to promote those measures designed to maintain and strengthen the family as the fundamental unit of society.

September 23, 1995

CHAPTER 30

CHILD ABUSE

Social workers, church leaders, ministers, police officers and others who work with children who are the victims of abuse sometimes go through a severe test themselves to control their anger and keep their basic respect for humanity. The Savior used some of His strongest language in condemning those who place stumbling blocks in the paths of children. In Matthew 18:5-6, we read:

> 5 And whoso shall receive one such little child in my name receiveth me. ¹

> 6 But whoso shall offend one of these little ones which believe in me, it were better for him that a millstone were hanged about his neck, and that he were drowned in the depth of the sea.

Tragically, there are many adults nowadays who seem to somehow rationalize themselves into feeling justified in abusing children. Satan is a master of deception. Such abuse comes in many forms. Therefore, it follows that Lucifer's dark deception comes in many forms, in order to successfully tempt the perpetrators to engage in their dark deeds. The Proclamation warns and testifies such that there can be no doubt as to the fate of child abusers. Repentance "nigh unto death" (Mosiah 27:28) is their only hope. They must face a mandatory Church disciplinary council in order to climb onto the road to forgiveness.

While many victims of child abuse successfully overcome this trauma and go on to lead normal lives, many do not. What happens to them? Did they get a fair chance here on earth? Will they ever be healed? How can they marry and lead a normal, happy family life? The answer to these and other questions is summed up in one simple phrase of eternal truth: God is fair.

How does this fairness come into play for those victims who never recover during this life? The answer is found in the Doctrine and Covenants. Speaking of the victims of other's evil deeds, the Lord said in D&C 50:7, "such shall be reclaimed." This is a straight forward, simple, comforting and powerful doctrine. From this, coupled with our knowledge of the Plan of Salvation, we come to understand that these individuals will be healed when they arrive in the spirit world. There they will have an opportunity to understand and live the gospel under completely fair circumstances. Between then and the final judgment day, which includes the Millennium and the ordinances done by proxies therein, they will have the opportunity to use their agency to complete all that is needed for their exaltation and eternal happiness. God is completely fair to all His children.

THE FAMILY

A PROCLAMATION TO THE WORLD

THE FIRST PRESIDENCY AND COUNCIL OF THE TWELVE APOSTLES

OF THE CHURCH OF JESUS CHRIST OF LATTER-DAY SAINTS

We, the First Presidency and the council of the Twelve Apostles of The Church of Jesus Christ of Latter-day Saints, solemnly proclaim that marriage between a man and a woman is ordained of God and that the family is central to the Creator's plan for the eternal destiny of His children.

All human beings—male and female—are created in the image of God. Each is a beloved spirit son or daughter of heavenly parents, and, as such, each has a divine nature and destiny. Gender is an essential characteristic of individual premortal, mortal, and eternal identity and purpose.

In the premortal realm, spirit sons and daughters knew and worshiped God as their eternal Father and accepted His plan by which His children could obtain a physical body and gain earthly experience to progress toward perfection and ultimately realize his or her divine destiny as an heir of eternal life. The divine plan of happiness enables family relationships to be perpetuated beyond the grave. Sacred ordinances and covenants available in holy temples make it possible for individuals to return to the presence of God and for families to be united eternally.

The first commandment that God gave to Adam and Eve pertained to their potential for parenthood as husband and wife. We declare that God's commandment for His children to multiply and replenish the earth remains in force. We further declare that God has commanded that the sacred powers of procreation are to be employed only between man and woman, lawfully wedded as husband and wife.

We declare the means by which mortal life is created to be divinely appointed. We affirm the sanctity of life and of its importance in God's eternal plan.

Husband and wife have a solemn responsibility to love and care for each other and for their children. "Children are an heritage of the Lord." (Psalms 127:3.)

Parents have a sacred duty to rear their children in love and righteousness, to provide for their physical and spiritual needs, to teach them to love and serve one another, to observe the commandments of God and to be law-abiding citizens wherever they live. Husbands and wives—mothers and fathers—will be held accountable before God for the discharge of these obligations.

The family is ordained of God. Marriage between man and woman is essential to His eternal plan. Children are entitled to birth within the bonds of matrimony, and to be reared by a father and a mother who honor marital vows with complete fidelity. Happiness in family life is most likely to be achieved when founded upon the teachings of the Lord Jesus Christ. Successful marriages and families are established and maintained on principles of faith, prayer, repentance, forgiveness, respect, love, compassion, work, and wholesome recreational activities. By divine design, fathers are to preside over their families in love and righteousness and are responsible to provide the necessities of life and protection of their families. Mothers are primarily responsible for the nurture of their children. In these sacred responsibilities, fathers and mothers are obligated to help one another as equal partners. Disability, death, or other circumstances may necessitate individual adaptation. Extended families should lend support when needed.

We warn that individuals who violate covenants of chastity, who abuse spouse or offspring, or who fail to fulfill family responsibilities will one day stand accountable before God. Further, **we warn that the disintegration of the family will bring upon individuals, communities, and nations the calamities foretold by ancient and modern prophets.**

We call upon responsible citizens and officers of government everywhere to promote those measures designed to maintain and strengthen the family as the fundamental unit of society.

September 23, 1995

CHAPTER 31

THE CAUSES OF LAST-DAYS CALAMITIES

This is pure prophecy. This is a prophecy that you can write in your journal and point out to children and grandchildren that you were alive when the Lord spoke this through His prophets and apostles. This may sound a bit dramatic, but it is absolutely true.

You may wish to read or reread some passages of scripture which provide considerable detail about the last-days "calamities foretold by ancient and modern prophets." Among many possibilities for your reading are:

Isaiah 59: 1-8	1 Timothy 4: 1-3	2 Timothy 3: 1-7
Matthew 24	JS-Matthew	D&C 29: 14-20
D&C 45: 15-29	D&C 88: 87-91	Revelation 6, 8, 9, 13, 16-18

(Note: For extra help in understanding Isaiah and also the references in the Book of Revelation, you may wish to read *Isaiah Made Easier* and *The New Testament Made Easier, Part 2*, by David J. Ridges).

Lest anyone get too worried and become pessimistic about living in these, the last days, we need but turn to our current prophet, President Gordon B. Hinckley, who constantly reminds us to be optimistic, to "be happy." Almost every time he speaks to his people, he says something to the effect of "what a wonderful time to be alive." In the Saturday morning session of the October 2001 General Conference of the Church, President Hinckley said:

"I do not know what we did in the preexistence to merit the wonderful blessings we enjoy. We have come to earth in this great season in the long history of mankind. It is a marvelous age, the best of all. As we reflect on the plodding course of mankind, from the time of our first parents, we cannot help feeling grateful."

This is one of the great prophetic messages and revelations of our time, the counsel and encouragement from God's living Prophet to look at the bright side and to not get caught up in the gloom and doom

105

resulting from no-holds-barred sin. What better way to avoid getting caught up in the pessimism and gloom of these last days than to follow the counsel and learn the doctrines taught in the Proclamation.

A PROCLAMATION TO THE WORLD

THE FIRST PRESIDENCY AND COUNCIL OF THE TWELVE APOSTLES
OF THE CHURCH OF JESUS CHRIST OF LATTER-DAY SAINTS

We, the First Presidency and the council of the Twelve Apostles of The Church of Jesus Christ of Latter-day Saints, solemnly proclaim that marriage between a man and a woman is ordained of God and that the family is central to the Creator's plan for the eternal destiny of His children.

All human beings—male and female—are created in the image of God. Each is a beloved spirit son or daughter of heavenly parents, and, as such, each has a divine nature and destiny. Gender is an essential characteristic of individual premortal, mortal, and eternal identity and purpose.

In the premortal realm, spirit sons and daughters knew and worshiped God as their eternal Father and accepted His plan by which His children could obtain a physical body and gain earthly experience to progress toward perfection and ultimately realize his or her divine destiny as an heir of eternal life. The divine plan of happiness enables family relationships to be perpetuated beyond the grave. Sacred ordinances and covenants available in holy temples make it possible for individuals to return to the presence of God and for families to be united eternally.

The first commandment that God gave to Adam and Eve pertained to their potential for parenthood as husband and wife. We declare that God's commandment for His children to multiply and replenish the earth remains in force. We further declare that God has commanded that the sacred powers of procreation are to be employed only between man and woman, lawfully wedded as husband and wife.

We declare the means by which mortal life is created to be divinely appointed. We affirm the sanctity of life and of its importance in God's eternal plan.

Husband and wife have a solemn responsibility to love and care for each other and for their children. "Children are an heritage of the Lord." (Psalms 127:3.)

Parents have a sacred duty to rear their children in love and righteousness, to provide for their physical and spiritual needs, to teach them to love and serve one another, to observe the commandments of God and to be law-abiding citizens wherever they live. Husbands and wives—mothers and fathers—will be held accountable before God for the discharge of these obligations.

The family is ordained of God. Marriage between man and woman is essential to His eternal plan. Children are entitled to birth within the bonds of matrimony, and to be reared by a father and a mother who honor marital vows with complete fidelity. Happiness in family life is most likely to be achieved when founded upon the teachings of the Lord Jesus Christ. Successful marriages and families are established and maintained on principles of faith, prayer, repentance, forgiveness, respect, love, compassion, work, and wholesome recreational activities. By divine design, fathers are to preside over their families in love and righteousness and are responsible to provide the necessities of life and protection of their families. Mothers are primarily responsible for the nurture of their children. In these sacred responsibilities, fathers and mothers are obligated to help one another as equal partners. Disability, death, or other circumstances may necessitate individual adaptation. Extended families should lend support when needed.

We warn that individuals who violate covenants of chastity, who abuse spouse or offspring, or who fail to fulfill family responsibilities will one day stand accountable before God. Further, we warn that the disintegration of the family will bring upon individuals, communities, and nations the calamities foretold by ancient and modern prophets.

We call upon responsible citizens and officers of government everywhere to promote those measures designed to maintain and strengthen the family as the fundamental unit of society.

September 23, 1995

CHAPTER 32

THE RESPONSIBILITY OF CITIZENS AND GOVERNMENT OFFICIALS TO STRENGTHEN THE FAMILY

Having been taught correct principles in "The Family: A Proclamation to the World," it now becomes the responsibility of citizens and governments in all the world to follow them. We are included in this group. Amos 3:7 says, "Surely the Lord GOD will do nothing, but he revealeth his secret unto his servants the prophets." He has revealed his "secret" to "his servants the prophets" and they have done what prophets, seers, and revelators have always done, namely, told us and the world what they have seen as "watchmen on the tower."

Members of the Church are not the only ones who have expressed concerns about the disintegration of the traditional family. Many from other Christian faiths as well as a great number from Arabic nations and others have joined with the Church in world conferences on the family to defend and explain the need to "maintain and strengthen the family as the fundamental unit of society."

What we do in our own homes, what we do in our personal spheres of influence in the neighborhood, the community, and the nation, all become a part of a "ripple effect" which spreads out from each of us to the rest of the world. We each touch many lives as instruments in the hand of the Lord. May we not underestimate our own humble efforts to "maintain and strengthen the family as the fundamental unit of society."

OTHER PROCLAMATIONS

Quite often, members ask "Are there any other 'Proclamations' from the Brethren?" The answer is "Yes." An excerpt from *Encyclopedia of Mormonism* is given here for your information.

Proclamations Of The First Presidency And The Quorum Of The Twelve Apostles

Encyclopedia of Mormonism, Vol.3, Proclamations of the First Presidency and the Quorum of the Twelve Apostles

In performance of their calling as apostles, prophets, seers, revelators, and spokesmen for The Church of Jesus Christ of Latter-day Saints, the First Presidency and the Quorum of the Twelve Apostles have from time to time issued formal written proclamations, declarations, letters, and various public announcements. These have been addressed sometimes to the members of the Church (as a type of general epistle) and sometimes to the public at large.

All such declarations have been solemn and sacred in nature and were issued with the intent to bring forth, build up, and regulate the affairs of the Church as the kingdom of God on the earth. Subject matter has included instruction on doctrine, faith, and history; warnings of judgments to come; invitations to assist in the work; and statements of Church growth and progress.

Only a few of the many formal declarations have been labeled "Proclamations." Others have been characterized "Official Declarations," "Doctrinal Expositions," or "Epistles." Some have the signature of the First Presidency, some of the First Presidency and the Twelve, and some of the Twelve only. This article considers four documents:

1. Proclamation of the First Presidency on January 15, 1841, at Nauvoo, Illinois.

2. Proclamation of the Twelve Apostles on April 6, 1845, in New York City, and on October 22, 1845, in Liverpool, England.

3. Proclamation of the First Presidency and the Twelve Apostles on October 21, 1865, in Salt Lake City, Utah.

4. Proclamation from the First Presidency and the Quorum of the Twelve Apostles, April 6, 1980, issued from Fayette, New York.

1. A Proclamation of the First Presidency of the Church to the Saints Scattered Abroad (January 15, 1841, Nauvoo, Illinois)

[This document, signed by Joseph Smith, Sidney Rigdon, and Hyrum Smith, reviews the progress of the Church in spite of hardships and persecution, and speaks at length on the prospects of the settlement of Nauvoo, as the following excerpts illustrate.]

Beloved brethren:—The relationship which we sustain to The Church of Jesus Christ of Latter-day Saints, renders it necessary that we should make known from time to time, the circumstances, situation, and prospects of the Church, and give such instructions as may be necessary for the well being of the Saints, and for the promotion of those objects calculated to further their present and everlasting happiness.

We have to congratulate the Saints on the progress of the great work of the "last days," for not only has it spread through the length and breadth of this vast continent, but on the continent of Europe, and on the islands of the sea, it is spreading in a manner entirely unprecedented in the annals of time. This appears the more pleasing when we consider, that but a short time has elapsed since we were unmercifully driven from the state of Missouri, after suffering cruelties and persecutions in various and horrid forms. . . .

It would be impossible to enumerate all those who, in our time of deep distress, nobly came forward to our relief, and, like the good Samaritan, poured oil into our wounds, and contributed liberally to our necessities, and the citizens of Quincy en masse, and the people of Illinois, generally, seemed to emulate each other in this labor of love. . . .

We would likewise make mention of the legislators of this state, who, without respect to parties, without reluctance, freely, openly, boldly, and nobly, have come forth to our assistance, owned us as citizens and friends, and took us by the hand, and extended to us all the blessings of civil, political, and religious liberty, by granting us, under date of December 16, 1840, one of the most liberal charters, with the most plenary powers ever conferred by a legislative assembly on free citizens, "The City of Nauvoo," the "Nauvoo Legion," and the "University of the City of Nauvoo." . . .

The name of our city (Nauvoo) is of Hebrew origin, and signifies a beautiful situation, or place, carrying with it, also, the idea of rest; and is truly descriptive of the most delightful location. It is situated on the east back of the Mississippi river, at the head of the Des Moines rapids, in Hancock county, bounded on the east by an extensive prairie of surpassing beauty, and on the north, west, and south, by the Mississippi. . . .

Having been instrumental, in the hands of our heavenly Father, in laying a foundation for the gathering of Zion, we would say, let all those who appreciate the blessings of the Gospel, and realize the importance of obeying the commandments of heaven, who have been blessed with the possession of this world's goods, first prepare for the general gathering; let them dispose of their effects as fast as circumstances will possibly admit, without making too great sacrifices, and remove to our city and county; establish and build up manufactures in the city, purchase and cultivate farms in the county. This will secure our permanent inheritance, and prepare the way for the gathering of the poor. This is agreeable to the order of heaven, and the only principle on which the gathering can be effected. Let the rich, then, and all who can assist in establishing this place, make every preparation to come on without delay, and strengthen our hands, and assist in promoting the happiness of the Saints. . . .

The Temple of the Lord is in process of erection here, where the Saints will come to worship the God of their fathers, according to the order of His house and the power of the Holy Priesthood, and will be so constructed as to enable all the functions of the Priesthood to be duly exercised, and where instructions from the Most High will be received, and from this place go forth to distant lands. Let us then concentrate all our powers, under the provisions of our magna charta granted by the Illinois legislature, at the "City of Nauvoo" and surrounding country, and strive to emulate the action of the ancient covenant fathers and Patriarchs, in those things which are of such vast importance to this and every succeeding generation. . . .

The greatest temporal and spiritual blessings which always flow from faithfulness and concerted effort, never attended individual exertion or enterprise. The history of all past ages abundantly attests this fact. In addition to all temporal blessings, there is no other way for the Saints to be saved in these last days [than by the gathering], as the concurrent testimony of all the holy Prophets clearly proves, for it is written—"They shall come from the east, and be gathered from the west; the north shall give up, and the south shall keep not back." "The sons of God shall be gathered from far, and His daughters from the ends of the earth."

It is also the concurrent testimony of all the Prophets, that this gathering together of all the Saints, must take place before the Lord comes to "take vengeance upon the ungodly," and to be glorified and admired by all those who obey the Gospel." The fiftieth Psalm, from the first to the fifth verse inclusive, describes the glory and majesty of that event.

The mighty God, and even the Lord hath spoken, and called the earth from the rising of the sun unto the going down thereof. Out of Zion, the perfection of beauty, God hath shined. Our God shall come and shall not keep silence; a fire shall devour before Him, and it shall be very tempestuous round about Him. He shall call to the heavens from above, and to the earth (that He may judge the people). Gather my Saints together unto me; those that have made covenant with me by sacrifice.

We might offer many other quotations from the Scriptures, but believing them to be familiar to the Saints, we forbear.

We would wish the Saints to understand that, when they come here, they must not expect perfection, or that all will be harmony, peace, and love; if they indulge these ideas, they will undoubtedly be deceived, for here there are persons, not only from different states, but from different nations, who, although they feel a great attachment to the cause of truth, have their prejudices of education, and, consequently, it requires some time before these things can be overcome. . . . Therefore, let those who come up to this place be determined to keep the commandments of God, and not be discouraged by those things we have enumerated, and then they will be prospered—the intelligence of heaven will be communicated to them, and they will eventually, see eye to eye, and rejoice in the full fruition of that glory which is reserved for the righteous.

In order to erect the Temple of the Lord, great exertions will be required on the part of the Saints, so that they may build a house which shall be accepted by the Almighty, in which His power and glory shall be manifested. Therefore let those who can freely make a sacrifice of their time, their talents, and their property, for the prosperity of the kingdom, and for the love they have to the cause of truth, bid adieu to their homes and pleasant places of abode, and unite with us in the great work of the last days, and share in the tribulation, that they may ultimately share in the glory and triumph.

We wish it likewise to be distinctly understood, that we claim no privilege but what we feel cheerfully disposed to share with our fellow citizens of every denomination, and every sentiment of religion; and therefore say, that so far from being restricted to our own faith, let all those who desire to locate themselves in this place, or the vicinity, come, and we will hail them as citizens and friends, and shall feel it not only a duty, but a privilege, to reciprocate the kindness we have received from the benevolent and kind-hearted citizens of the state of Illinois.

Joseph Smith,
Sidney Rigdon,
Hyrum Smith,
Presidents of the Church
[HC 4:267-73]

2. Proclamation of the Twelve Apostles of The Church of Jesus Christ of Latter-day Saints (April 6 and October 22, 1845)

[The Proclamation of 1845 was issued by the Twelve only, because at that time there was no First Presidency due to the martyrdom of the Prophet Joseph Smith on June 27, 1844, and a new First Presidency was not organized until December 1847. The Proclamation was apparently made in response to a revelation given January 19, 1841 (D&C 124:1-11). It was first printed in a sixteen-page pamphlet in New York City on April 6, 1845, and again in Liverpool, England, October 22, 1845. It was addressed to the rulers and people of all nations. This document was an announcement that God had spoken from the heavens and had restored the gospel of Jesus Christ to the earth. It spoke of blessings and of punishments to come, issued a warning voice, and invited all who were interested to assist in the building of the kingdom of God on the earth in preparation for the Savior's second coming. On October 3, 1975, President Ezra Taft Benson, president of the Quorum of the Twelve Apostles, spoke of this Proclamation and quoted portions of it in his general conference address (Ensign 15 [Oct. 1975]:32-34). Extracts from the 1845 Proclamation follow.]

TO ALL THE KINGS OF THE WORLD, TO THE PRESIDENT OF THE UNITED STATES OF AMERICA; TO THE GOVERNORS OF THE SEVERAL STATES, AND TO THE RULERS AND PEOPLE OF ALL NATIONS.

Greeting.

Know ye that the kingdom of God has come, as has been predicted by ancient prophets, and prayed for in all ages; even that kingdom which shall fill the whole earth, and shall stand for ever. . . .

Therefore we send unto you, with authority from on high, and command you all to repent and humble yourselves as little children before the majesty of the Holy One; and come unto Jesus with a broken heart and a contrite spirit, and be baptized in his name for the remission of sins (that is, be buried in the water, in the likeness of his burial, and rise again to newness of life in the likeness of his resurrection), and you shall receive the gift of the Holy Spirit, through the laying on of the hands of the apostles and elders, of this great and last dispensation of mercy to man.

This Spirit shall bear witness to you of the truth of our testimony, and shall enlighten your minds, and be in you as the spirit of prophecy and revelation; it shall bring things past to your understanding and remembrance, and shall show you things to come. . . .

By the light of this Spirit, received through the ministration of the ordinances—by the power and authority of the Holy Apostleship and Priesthood, you will be enabled to understand, and to be the children of light; and thus be prepared to escape all the things that are coming on the earth, and so stand before the Son of Man.

We testify that the foregoing doctrine is the doctrine or gospel of Jesus Christ in its fulness; and that it is the only true, everlasting, and unchangeable gospel; and the only plan revealed on earth whereby man can be saved. . . .

And we further testify that the Lord has appointed a holy city and temple to be built on this continent, for the Endowment and ordinances pertaining to the priesthood; and for the Gentiles, and the remnant of Israel to resort unto, in order to worship the Lord, and to be taught in his ways and walk in his paths; in short, to finish their preparations for the coming of the Lord. . . .

The Latter-day Saints, since their first organization in the year 1830, have been a poor, persecuted, abused, and afflicted people. They have sacrificed their time and property freely, for the sake of laying the foundation of the kingdom of God, and enlarging its dominion by the ministry of the gospel. They have suffered privation, hunger, imprisonment, and the loss of houses, lands, home, and political rights for their testimony.

And this is not all. Their first founder, Mr. Joseph Smith, whom God raised up as a prophet and apostle, mighty in word and in deed, and his brother Hyrum, who was also a prophet, together with many others, have suffered a cruel martyrdom in the cause of truth, and have sealed their testimony with their blood; and still the work has, as it were, but just begun.

A great, a glorious, and a mighty work is yet to be achieved, in spreading the truth and kingdom among the Gentiles—in restoring, organizing, instructing and establishing the Jews—in gathering, instructing, relieving, civilizing, educating, and administering salvation to the remnant of Israel on this continent—in building Jerusalem in Palestine, and the cities, stakes, temples, and sanctuaries of Zion in America; and in gathering the Gentiles into the same covenant and organization—instructing them in all things for their sanctification and preparation, that the whole Church of the Saints, both Gentile, Jew and Israel, may be prepared as a bride for the coming of the Lord. . . .

Again, we say, by the word of the Lord, to the people as well as to the rulers, your aid and your assistance is required in this great work; and you are hereby invited, in the name of Jesus, to take an active part in it from this day forward.

Open your churches, doors, and hearts for the truth; hear the apostles and elders of the Church of the Saints when they come into your cities and neighbourhoods; read and search the scriptures carefully, and see whether these things are so; read the publications of the Saints, and help to publish them to others; seek for the witness of the Spirit, and come and obey the glorious fulness of the gospel, and help us to build the cities and sanctuaries of our God. . . .

To this city [Zion or New Jerusalem], and to its several branches or stakes, shall the Gentiles seek, as to a standard of light and knowledge; yea, the nations, and their kings and nobles shall say—Come, and let us go up to the Mount Zion, and to the temple of the Lord, where his holy priesthood stand to minister continually before the Lord; and where we may be instructed more fully, and receive the ordinances of remission, and of sanctification, and redemption, and thus be adopted into the family of Israel, and identified in the same covenants of promise. . . .

The city of Zion, with its sanctuary and priesthood, and the glorious fulness of the gospel, will constitute a standard which will put an end to jarring creeds and political wranglings, by uniting the republics, states, provinces, territories, nations, tribes, kindred, tongues, people, and sects of North and South America in one great and common bond of brotherhood; while truth and knowledge shall make them free, and love cement their union.

The Lord also shall be their king and their lawgiver; while wars shall cease and peace prevail for a thousand years. . . .

We say, then, in life or in death, in bonds or free, that the great God has spoken in this age.—And we know it.

He has given us the holy priesthood and apostleship, and the keys of the kingdom of God, to bring about the restoration of all things as promised by the holy prophets of old.—And we know it.

He has revealed the origin and the records of the aboriginal tribes of America, and their future destiny.—And we know it.

He has revealed the fulness of the gospel, with its gifts, blessings, and ordinances.—And we know it. . . .

He has commanded us to gather together his Saints, on this continent, and build up holy cities and sanctuaries.—And we know it.

He has said, that the Gentiles should come into the same gospel and covenant, and be numbered with the house of Israel, and be a blessed people upon this good land for ever, if they would repent and embrace it.—And we know it. . . .

He has said, that the time is at hand for the Jews to be gathered to Jerusalem.—And we know it.

He has said, that the ten tribes of Israel should also be revealed in the north country, together with their oracles and records, preparatory to their return, and to their union with Judah, no more to be separated.—And we know it.

He has said, that when these preparations were made, both in this country and in Jerusalem, and the gospel in all its fulness preached to all nations for a witness and testimony, he will come, and all the Saints with him, to reign on the earth one thousand years.—And we know it.

He has said, that he will not come in his glory and destroy the wicked, till these warnings were given, and these preparations were made for his reception.—And we know it. . . .

Therefore, again we say to all people, repent, and be baptized in the name of Jesus Christ, for remission of sins, and you shall receive the Holy Spirit, and shall know the truth, and be numbered with the house of Israel. . . .

New York, April 6th, 1845
TO THE ENGLISH READER.

It will be borne in mind that the foregoing was written in the United States of America, therefore the language, which we have not altered, will be understood as emanating from thence. . . .

W. Woodruff.
Liverpool, October 22nd, 1845

[Liverpool pamphlet, BYU Library, Provo, Utah: see also James R. Clark, *Messages of the First Presidency*, comp., 5 vols. Salt Lake City, 1965-1975, vol. 1:252-66].

(*Encyclopedia of Mormonism*, Vol. 3, Proclamations of the First Presidency and the Quorum of the Twelve Apostles.)

3. Proclamation of the First Presidency and the Twelve Apostles (October 21, 1865)

[This document was issued to members of the Church to correct certain theories about the nature of God that had been published by one of the Twelve in official Church literature, without having those statements cleared and verified by the First Presidency and the Twelve.

An apparent major purpose of this Proclamation was to emphasize the established order of the Church, that new doctrine is to be announced only by the First Presidency. A paragraph near the end of the Proclamation states:]

It ought to have been known, years ago, by every person in the Church—for ample teachings have been given on the point—that no member of the Church has the right to publish any doctrines, as the doctrines of the Church of Jesus Christ of Latter-day Saints, without first submitting them for examination and approval to the First Presidency and the Twelve. There is but one man upon the earth, at one time, who holds the keys to receive commandments and revelations for the Church, and who has the authority to write doctrines by way of commandment unto the Church. And any man who so far forgets the order instituted by the Lord as to write and publish what may be termed new doctrines, without consulting with the First Presidency of the Church respecting them, places himself in a false position, and exposes himself to the power of darkness by violating his Priesthood. (James R. Clark, *Messages of the First Presidency*, comp., 5 vols. Salt Lake City, 1965-1975, vol. 2:239)

[The Proclamation is signed by Brigham Young, Heber C. Kimball, Orson Hyde, John Taylor, Wilford Woodruff, George A. Smith, Amasa M. Lyman, Ezra T. Benson, Charles C. Rich, Lorenzo Snow, Erastus Snow, Franklin D. Richards, and George Q. Cannon.]

4. Proclamation of the First Presidency and the Quorum of the Twelve Apostles of The Church of Jesus Christ of Latter-day Saints (April 6, 1980)

(This document was put forth in commemoration of the 150th anniversary of the organization of the Church. On Sunday, April 6, 1980, a portion of the Sunday morning session of General Conference was broadcast from the newly reconstructed Peter Whitmer, Sr., home in Fayette, New York. President Spencer W. Kimball spoke briefly of the organization of the Church that had occurred on that very spot of ground. He then announced that the Church had a proclamation to declare. President Kimball's concluding words were as follows:)

Now, my brothers and sisters, with the future before us, and sensing deeply the responsibilities and divine mission of the restored Church on this sacred occasion, the First Presidency and the Quorum of the Twelve Apostles declare to the world a proclamation. We have felt it appropriate to issue this statement from here, where the Church began. Accordingly, I shall ask Elder Gordon B. Hinckley of the Quorum of the Twelve Apostles, to speak in my behalf and in behalf of my brethren, to read this proclamation to you and to the world (*Conference Report*, April 1980, p. 74.)

Elder Gordon B. Hinckley then read the Proclamation from the Whitmer home in Fayette, New York, which was broadcast by satellite to the Tabernacle in Salt Lake City, and published in the April 12, 1980 Church News, in the May 1980 Ensign, and in the April 1980 Conference Report. The full text of the proclamation follows.

The Church of Jesus Christ of Latter-day Saints was organized 150 years ago today. On this sesquicentennial anniversary we issue to the world a proclamation concerning its progress, its doctrine, its mission, and its message.

On April 6, 1830, a small group assembled in the farmhouse of Peter Whitmer in Fayette Township in the State of New York. Six men participated in the formal organization procedures, with Joseph Smith as their leader. From that modest beginning in a rural area, this work has grown consistently and broadly, as men and women in many lands have embraced the doctrine and entered the waters of baptism. There are now almost four and a half million living members, and the Church is stronger and growing more rapidly than at any time in its history. Congregations of Latter-day Saints are found throughout North, Central, and South America; in the nations of Europe; in Asia; in Africa; in Australia and the islands of the South Pacific; and in other areas of the world. The gospel restored through the instrumentality of Joseph Smith is presently taught in forty-six languages and in eighty-one nations. From that small meeting held in a farmhouse a century and a half ago, the Church has grown until today it includes nearly 12,000 organized congregations.

We testify that this restored gospel was introduced into the world by the marvelous appearance of God the Eternal Father and His Son, the resurrected Lord Jesus Christ. That most glorious manifestation marked the beginning of the fulfillment of the promise of Peter, who prophesied of "the times of restitution of all things, which God hath spoken by the mouth of all his holy prophets since the world began," this in preparation for the coming of the Lord to reign personally upon the earth (Acts 3:21).

We solemnly affirm that The Church of Jesus Christ of Latter-day Saints is in fact a restoration of the Church established by the Son of God, when in mortality he organized his work upon the earth; that it carries his sacred name, even the name of Jesus Christ; that it is built upon a foundation of Apostles and prophets, he being the chief corner-stone; that its priesthood, in both the Aaronic and Melchizedek orders, was restored under the hands of those who held it anciently: John the Baptist, in the case of the Aaronic; and Peter, James, and John in the case of the Melchizedek.

We declare that the Book of Mormon was brought forth by the gift and power of God and that it stands beside the Bible as another witness of Jesus the Christ, the Savior and Redeemer of mankind. Together they testify of his divine sonship.

We give our witness that the doctrines and practices of the Church encompass salvation and exaltation not only for those who are living, but also for the dead, and that in sacred temples built for this purpose a great vicarious work is going forward in behalf of those who have died, so that all men and women of all generations may become the beneficiaries of the saving ordinances of the gospel of the Master. This great, selfless labor is one of the distinguishing features of this restored Church of Jesus Christ.

We affirm the sanctity of the family as a divine creation and declare that God our Eternal Father will hold parents accountable to rear their children in light and truth, teaching them "to pray, and to walk uprightly before the Lord" (D&C 68:28). We teach that the most sacred of all relationships, those family associations of husbands and wives and parents and children, may be continued eternally when marriage is solemnized under the authority of the holy priesthood exer-cised in temples dedicated for these divinely authorized purposes.

We bear witness that all men and women are sons and daughters of God, each accountable to him; that our lives here on earth are part of an eternal plan; that death is not the end, but rather a transition from this to another sphere of purposeful activity made possible through the Atonement of the Redeemer of the world; and that we shall there have the opportunity of working and growing toward perfection.

We testify that the spirit of prophecy and revelation is among us. "We believe all that God has revealed, all that He does now reveal; and we believe that He will yet reveal many great and important things pertaining to the Kingdom of God" (Articles of Faith 1:9). The heavens are not sealed; God continues to speak to his children through a prophet empowered to declare his word, now as he did anciently.

The mission of the Church today, as it has been from the beginning, is to teach the gospel of Christ to all the world in obedience to the commandment given by the Savior prior to his ascension and repeated in modern revelation: "Go ye into all the world, preach the gospel to every creature, acting in the authority which I have given you, baptizing in the name of the Father, and of the Son, and of the Holy Ghost" (D&C 68:8).

Through the Prophet Joseph Smith the Lord revealed these words of solemn warning:

Hearken ye people from afar; and ye that are upon the islands of the sea, listen together. For verily, the voice of the Lord is unto all men, and there is none to escape; and there is no eye that shall not see, neither ear that shall not hear, neither heart that shall not be penetrated. And the rebellious shall be pierced with much sorrow; for their iniquities shall be spoken upon the housetops, and their secret acts shall be revealed. And the voice of warning shall be unto all people, by the mouths of my disciples, whom I have chosen in these last days (D&C 1:1-4).

It is our obligation, therefore, to teach faith in the Lord Jesus Christ, to plead with the people of the earth for individual repentance, to administer the sacred ordinances of baptism by immersion for the remission of sins and the laying on of hands for the gift of the Holy Ghost—all of this under the authority of the priesthood of God.

It is our responsibility to espouse and follow an inspired program of instruction and activity, and to build and maintain appropriate facilities for the accomplishment of this, that all who will hear and accept may grow in understanding of doctrine and develop in principles of Christian service to their fellowmen.

As we stand today on the summit of 150 years of progress, we contemplate humbly and gratefully the sacrifices of those who have gone before us, many of whom gave their lives in testimony of this truth. We are thankful for their faith, for their example, for their mighty labors and willing consecrations for this cause which they considered more precious than life itself. They have passed to us a remarkable heritage. We are resolved to build on that heritage for the blessing and benefit of those who follow, who will constitute ever enlarging numbers of faithful men and women throughout the earth.

This is God's work. It is his kingdom we are building. Anciently the prophet Daniel spoke of it as a stone cut out of the mountain without hands, which was to roll forth to fill the whole earth (see Dan. 2:31-45). We invite the honest in heart everywhere to listen to the teachings of our missionaries who are sent forth as messengers of eternal truth, to study and learn, and to ask God, our Eternal Father, in the name of his Son, the Lord Jesus Christ, if these things are true.

> And if ye shall ask with a sincere heart, with real intent, having faith in Christ, he will manifest the truth of it unto you, by the power of the Holy Ghost. And by the power of the Holy Ghost ye may know the truth of all things (Moro. 10:4-5)

We call upon all men and women to forsake evil and turn to God; to work together to build that brotherhood which must be recognized when we truly come to know that God is our Father and we are his children; and to worship him and his Son, the Lord Jesus Christ, the Savior of mankind. In the authority of the Holy Priesthood in us vested, we bless the seekers of truth wherever they may be and invoke the favor of the Almighty upon all men and nations whose God is the Lord, in the name of Jesus Christ, amen. [*Conference Report*, April 1980, pp. 75-77; see also *Ensign* (May 1980):51-53]

ABOUT THE AUTHOR

David J. Ridges

David J. Ridges has been teaching for the Church Educational System for 35 years and has taught for several years at BYU Campus Education Week and Know Your Religion programs. He has also served as a curriculum writer for Sunday School, Seminary, and Institute of Religion manuals. He is also the author of the best-selling *Gospel Studies Series*, an in-depth study of the Standard Works of the LDS Church

He has served in many positions in the Church, including gospel doctrine teacher, bishop, stake president and patriarch.

Brother Ridges and his wife, Janette, are the parents of six children and make their home in Springville, Utah.

0 26575 77166 4